D1010833

Leading the
LEARNING
Revolution

Leading the
LEARNING
Revolution

The Expert's Guide to
Capitalizing on the Exploding
Lifelong Education Market

Jeff Cobb

AMACOM

American Management Association
New York • Atlanta • Brussels • Chicago • Mexico City • San Francisco
Shanghai • Tokyo • Toronto • Washington, D.C.

Bulk discounts available. For details visit:
www.amacombooks.org/go/specialsales
Or contact special sales:
Phone: 800-250-5308
Email: specialsls@amanet.org
View all the AMACOM titles at: www.amacombooks.org
American Management Association: 222.amanet.org

This publication is designed to provide accurate and authoritative information in regard to the subject matter covered. It is sold with the understanding that the publisher is not engaged in rendering legal, accounting, or other professional service. If legal advice or other expert assistance is required, the services of a competent professional person should be sought.

Library of Congress Cataloging-in-Publication Data

Cobb, Jeff.
    Leading the learning revolution : the expert's guide to capitalizing on the exploding lifelong education market / Jeff Cobb.
        p.   cm.
    Includes index.
    ISBN 978-0-8144-3225-9 — ISBN 0-8144-3225-5   1. Continuing education—Marketing.   2. Adult education—Marketing.   3. Education and training services industry.   I. Title.
    LC5225.M37C63   2013
    374—dc23

                                                                    2012032413

About AMA
American Management Association (www.amanet.org) is a world leader in talent development, advancing the skills of individuals to drive business success. Our mission is to support the goals of individuals and organizations through a complete range of products and services, including classroom and virtual seminars, webcasts, webinars, podcasts, conferences, corporate and government solutions, business books, and research. AMA's approach to improving performance combines experiential learning—learning through doing—with opportunities for ongoing professional growth at every step of one's career journey.

Printing number
10 9 8 7 6 5 4 3 2 1

In memory of
William Chapman
and
Vermell Cobb

CONTENTS

ACKNOWLEDGMENTS

No book like this gets written without the benefit of much experience. I am grateful to Elizabeth Kellison, Alec Hudnut, and Tom Geniesse for opening the door many years ago that led to where I am today, and to the many clients and colleagues who have since provided me with opportunities to learn and grow along the way.

To David Houle—friend, colleague, mentor, and collaborator: Thanks for helping to light the path.

Thank you to my association community colleagues Ned Campbell, Colleen Cunningham, Lloyd Tucker, and Dave Will for taking the time to share their experiences.

Thank you to Seth Kahan, Dorie Clark, and the other members of Alan Weiss' community—including Alan himself—who took the time to talk with me about the book and share their insights.

A special thanks to Leo Babauta, Howie Jacobson, Tom Kuhlman, Kristie McDonald, Monisha Pasupathi, George Siemens, and Michael Stelzner, none of whom knew me from Adam before I contacted them about doing an interview for this book, but were kind enough to make the time all the same.

To Emily Wilson, thank you for the use of your little house at Swansboro as a welcome writer's retreat. Ed, thanks for helping to arrange that, and Laurie and Buddy, thank you for being willing to provide a great example from everyday life.

And thank you, finally, to Celisa, simply for being there and being who you are.

YOUR OPPORTUNITY, SHOULD YOU CHOOSE TO ACCEPT IT

THIS BOOK is based on three straightforward ideas.

The first is that we live in a world that is more connected and changes faster day in and day out than has ever been the case before.

The second is that to thrive in this world, we must continually develop new knowledge and skills. Never before has ongoing, effective lifelong learning been so necessary for so many people both as a path to economic success and simply for making sense of and finding fulfillment in a highly complex world.

The third is that technology has reached a tipping point in the past few years. Not only are there many more ways to deliver education outside the traditional classroom; the technologies are dramatically less expensive, easier to use, and much more broadly embraced by the public than they were as little as a decade ago.

These three ideas together suggest a tremendous opportunity: We are at a point at which nearly anyone with a decent computer, a high-speed Internet connection, and expertise or access to expertise in a topic or skill set can reach a global audience in very sophisticated ways.

That "anyone" may very well be you.

Depending on your background and your perspective, little of this may seem like news, but consider what the situation was just a little over a decade ago.

In the go-go dot-com 1990s, I worked for a start-up e-learning company whose founders had a vision for capturing lectures from top-ranked schools and distributing them into community colleges and second-tier universities. The idea was to provide access to a caliber of content that students at these institutions might not otherwise get. It was a compelling vision, and the company produced some wonderful educational content. To do this, though, was no small matter. We spent millions on high-end audio and video equipment and the talent to go with it so that we could capture lectures. We paid dozens of Flash and HTML programmers to create interactive web content and employed teams of writers, graphic artists, and editors to create great text and visual content. Much of my own work involved traveling from business school to business school to secure complex contracts for the professors who would deliver the lectures. My colleagues and I were certain we had found a model that was going to transform the world of education. The market, however, was not so certain, and the sales we hoped for never materialized.

Of course, in those days it was all too easy to find and spend money on "the next big thing." When the venture fell apart, it was also easy to draw the conclusion that maybe the Internet and the whole concept of online education were not going to be all that the hype had made them out to be. By 2002, the bubble had burst, and the people at my company, and at countless other companies, had dispersed and gone off to work on other things. The revolution we had been a part of had seemingly fizzled.

Now, fast-forward a decade, and consider what has happened in the meantime.

◆ Many of the things we now consider a standard part of our Internet experience have come into existence only in this intervening decade—some only in the past five years. These include Google, YouTube, Facebook, iTunes, smartphones, and even low-cost, reliable web conferencing technologies, just to name a very few. Awareness and use of most of these technologies have become the norm in only the past few years, even if it now seems like they have been around forever.

◆   The global economic landscape has shifted dramatically. Thomas Friedman's landmark book *The World Is Flat: A Brief History of the Twenty-First Century*, published in 2005, captured the way in which the evaporation of economic borders has changed the nature of work forever. This point has been punctuated by the global recession that began in 2007 and from which the world has not yet fully emerged.

◆   With unemployment soaring, and rampant uncertainty now the norm across many labor markets, the focus on education has become more intense than at any point since the aftermath of World War II. There is widespread recognition that we need to better prepare people for the world we now live in, and we need to help those who have been displaced gain new knowledge and skills that will help them get back on track.

◆   The baby boomers, who represented the largest generation in history until their children came along, are starting to "retire." Retirement, however, is not what it used to be. Many boomers are shifting to second careers, whether out of interest or necessity. Others are taking advantage of their newly found freedom to engage in a wide variety of learning activities that they had no time for previously.

◆   Finally, online education has gone mainstream. Online courses are offered by every major college and university, as well as most smaller ones. E-learning is a standard part of corporate training departments, and more than 70 percent of trade and professional associations deliver at least some of their continuing education offerings online. At the time I am writing this book, Harvard and MIT have just announced a major new initiative to offer free, online college-level courses. This is just one of many "open" education initiatives from major institutions. As a *Boston Globe* article put it, "Online education is now a juggernaut; more than 6.1 million current college students took a web-based course in fall 2010. Nearly a third of students have taken one during their college careers."[1]

If I were to start a company now similar to the one that blew through so much money at the turn of this century, I could create and distribute substantially similar offerings for thousands rather than millions of dollars. Just as important, I would be offering these up to a global market that is now broadly familiar with and comfortable with a wide range of technologies and is hungry for acquiring new skills and knowledge. And that is precisely my point.

If you don't believe me, consider the case of Salman Khan, who single-handedly, using simple video and web tools, has produced more than 2,000 short videos on mathematics, economics, and a range of scientific topics. Khan was not a teacher. He was a very smart hedge fund manager who wanted to help his cousin with a topic he knew well. His Khan Academy now features more than 3,000 videos and as of this writing has delivered nearly 150 million lessons. Teachers, parents, students, and the general public have all embraced Khan's videos and are using them to supplement, complement, and eliminate traditional classroom education in a wide variety of ways. When you consider how slow the widespread adoption of technology in K–12 education has been, this represents a major disruption—largely sparked by the efforts of a single individual.

Or consider Leo Babauta. In 2005, Leo was a journalist and father of six living in Guam. Determined to change his life, Leo started writing about his efforts to adopt new, positive habits and shed ones that he felt were harmful. Leo's quest struck a chord, and by 2009 he had more than 50,000 subscribers to his blog, Zen Habits. That year he launched, in collaboration with Mary Jaksch, an online learning bootcamp and community to help others succeed with blogging. Again, using a relatively simple set of tools, and producing the initial content entirely on their own, Leo and Mary were able to launch a successful, vibrant membership community that generates significant income and continues to thrive and grow today.

Or Michael Stelzner. Stelzner started the highly successful online magazine *Social Media Examiner* just a few years ago to compete with rapidly growing blogs like Mashable. *Social Media Examiner* has been successful in attracting tens of thousands of readers, but the real core of the business model is the online events produced by the magazine. The biggest of these, the annual Social Media Success Summit, is an online virtual conference that leverages basic web conferencing technologies and the freely available LinkedIn social network to attract thousands of marketers—at a list price of $595 per ticket.

Finally, there is Udacity, a company that has sprung from the efforts of a professor at a top-ranked school to deliver his class to a much larger audience. Sound familiar? In late 2011, Sebastian Thrun and his colleague Peter Norvig offered a "massive open online course" (MOOC) through Stanford University on the topic of artificial intelligence. Lectures were recorded in a studio set up in the basement of Thrun's guesthouse with video equipment that is a significant step up from what Khan uses but still a far cry from hiring a professional video crew. The free Google Moderator tool was used to facilitate student participation and interaction. The result? More than 160,000 students from around the world enrolled in the free course. Thrun subsequently gave up his tenure at Stanford and went on to launch Udacity, where the plan is to replicate similar large-scale classes across a variety of topics.

These examples vary in their focus, their business models, and where they are along the path to creating successful businesses, but each is nothing less than revolutionary in its own way. Less than a decade ago they would have been extremely difficult, if not impossible, to achieve. Now they are within the grasp of anyone with entrepreneurial drive and access to expertise. For newcomers to the world of lifelong learning, this represents a huge opportunity. It is an opportunity for established learning providers as well—but also a wake-up call.

ARE YOU A REVOLUTIONARY?

This book is for any individual or any organization that sees the tremendous opportunities the market for lifelong learning now offers and wants a roadmap for pursuing those opportunities.

This includes anyone who possesses significant experience and expertise that they can share with others. Not just traditional trainers and teachers—though certainly you will find most of what follows very useful if you happen to fall into one of these categories—but also entrepreneurs, consultants, retirees, stay-at-home parents, passionate hobbyists, or anyone else who feels that the knowledge and skills they possess would be helpful to others.

It includes organizations like trade and professional associations, college and university continuing education programs, and even many businesses that play a role as brokers of expertise or that see valuable opportunities for playing this role.

In the chapters that follow, I provide a bit more background on how the market for lifelong learning has shifted and what forces are driving the change. I think it is important to appreciate the broader context before moving to the nuts and bolts of creating, running, and growing a lifelong learning business. For the majority of the book, however, I focus on the much more practical issues you will face as you capitalize on the market for your expertise. These include:

- Assessing and testing the market
- Developing a business model
- Positioning and pricing your offerings
- Designing high-value learning experiences
- Mastering the tools of the trade
- Marketing your offerings
- Keeping it all going over time
- What it means to *lead* learning

My goal is twofold: to help you build a profitable lifelong business that will continue to grow over time and to help you lead learning in your field, profession, or market. If this is a goal you share, let's get started.

NOTES

1. Mary Carmichael and Johanna Kaiser, "Harvard, MIT to partner in $60 million initiative to offer free online classes to all," May 2, 2012, http://www.boston.com/yourtown/cambridge/articles/ 2012/05/03/harvard_mit_to_partner_in_60_million_initiative_to_ offer_free_online_classes_to_all/. Retrieved July 5, 2012.

CHAPTER 1

THE NEW LEARNING LANDSCAPE

I'VE CHOSEN TO FOCUS this book on lifelong learning partly because that is my background—it is a market in which I have worked for well over a decade—but also because I think it has received surprisingly little attention in all of the excited and often heated discussion about education in the past several years. I take the term "lifelong learning" literally—it means learning that occurs throughout the life of an individual—but for the purposes of this book, I will focus on what I think of as "the other fifty years." So much of the broader public discussion about education focuses on the K–12 sector and higher education. But the reality for most people is that they will exit these systems with at least another fifty years ahead of them. To say there is a significant—and growing—need for learning during these years would be a vast understatement, and yet you rarely hear politicians, trade and professional association CEOs, college and university presidents, or other potential learning leaders articulate a compelling vision for how we should serve this huge market.

It is clear, however, that this market is changing—indeed, already has changed significantly—and part of what inspired me to write this book is the efforts I have seen by entrepreneurial thinkers over the past several years to fill in the gaps left by traditional approaches to continuing education and professional development. In this chapter, I examine five forces that I think are driving these gaps and discuss their impact on the business of lifelong learning. By their nature, the five forces are:

1. Economic
2. Educational
3. Technological
4. Neuropsychological
5. Generational

I believe these forces ensure that the market for lifelong learning will continue to grow dramatically and dynamically in the coming years.

THE LEARNING ECONOMY

The study of economics has offered many important lessons over the past two hundred years, but the one I find most important to education providers as we make our way into the twenty-first century is this: *The nature of work changes with increasing speed as economies mature.* To not recognize and actively address this fact is to wind up in a situation in which there is a significant gap between what businesses need and what the labor pool can provide. Indeed, that is where we find ourselves, both in the United States and many other developed economies, as I write this book.

A September 2011 article in the *Economist* argued that even as unemployment surges, businesses are having a difficult time finding people with the types and levels of talent they need for open positions. "[A] minority," the article suggests, "is benefitting from an intensifying war for talent. That minority is well placed to demand interesting and fulfilling work and set its own terms and conditions."[1] This minority, of course, is very well educated and highly capable of adapting to changing circumstances.

In retrospect, we have been evolving toward this point at an accelerating rate for centuries. In the early 1800s—a mere two hundred years ago—the vast majority of the U.S. population lived and worked on small farms or ran businesses that served the needs of farmers. The nature of work, even given a range of technical innovations, was not terribly different from what it had been for thousands of years before. Plant, harvest, process, sell, or do things to support these activities. Only a hundred years later the majority of the population lived in cities, and manufacturing had become the engine of our economy. The demands of this economy—both to do the work of manufacturing and to provide a food supply to support large numbers of people who no longer worked on farms—meant that a wide range of entirely new jobs were created and that the nature of the old jobs had to change significantly. As manufacturing grew and farming evolved, both became increasingly less labor intensive and more specialized in the types of labor involved. Just as important, with the spread of public and higher education and continuing advances in technology, there was a dramatic increase in the pace at which new types of jobs emerged, became increasingly specialized, and then either disappeared or adapted to yet more change.

Skip forward another hundred years, and both rural and industrial life are distant memories for most of us. For decades we have lived in what the prescient Peter Drucker dubbed a "knowledge economy," one driven by service- and information-based businesses. But just decades later, even Drucker's term no longer seems quite on the mark. "Knowledge" sounds too finite: Master a body of knowledge and you are on your way. There are professions where that still works, at least as a point of entry, but as any recent college graduate can attest, those professions and those points of entry are becoming harder and harder to find. We now live in what is not so much a "knowledge" economy but rather a "figure it out on a daily basis" economy. Or, more formally, a *learning economy*.

Many of us, even those who remain in the same jobs, see the nature of our work change from year to year, and sometimes much faster. Technology is one key driver of this continuous change; globalization is another. Most of us are now all too familiar with the idea that a software program or a lower-paid worker in another country may be able to do our work as well or better than we can. This knowledge, in and of itself, creates a perpetual uncertainty in the labor market. And most of us recognize that we are unlikely to remain in any one job for our entire careers or even for long stretches of time, as was the norm for previous generations.

Indeed, the Bureau of Labor Statistics of the U.S. Department of Labor indicates that the "average person born in the later years of the baby boom held 10.8 jobs from age 18 to age 42."[2] There is little, if any, reason to believe that this number will decline—unless, of course, the drop is driven by the grim fact that so many in the younger generations will be starting work later given the current lack of entry-level job openings. In addition to shifting jobs, many of us may also shift careers at least once during our working years. Either situation creates significant new learning demands.

Increasingly, for individuals, there are two options. One is to stick to the path of traditional employment, but to be as fully prepared as possible for the less secure environment that this path now offers. This is a particular challenge in professions in which the work lends itself to being codified and systematized, as is the case in a growing number of mid-level, white-collar positions. The process of off-shoring or computerizing any job that requires straightforward information processing—from insurance claims to bookkeeping to routine legal tasks—is already well under way. Assuming that robotics finally makes the leap that seems inevitable, the situation will become only more challenging. As technology futurist Kevin Kelly puts it, "Productivity is for machines. If you can measure it, robots should do it."[3]

While creativity, critical thinking, and leadership are often cited as aptitudes needed for combating this trend and securing coveted "high-talent" jobs, I'd argue that these are not enough. These aptitudes, valuable as they are, require continual replenishment through learning. Individuals who hope to survive, much less thrive, in traditional employment in the learning economy must actively pursue educational opportunities that maintain their value to their employers. In many cases, if not most, this will mean seeking opportunities that fall outside of whatever education and training the employer offers.

The other option is to throw off the reins of traditional employment and set out on your own. This is no silver bullet, of course: Individuals who choose this path need all of the same aptitudes and the drive to learn that their more traditional peers need, but they must also have the courage and the discipline to be self-reliant. Whether by choice or force of circumstance, an increasing number of individuals are, in fact, choosing this path. A 2011 series in the *Atlantic* points to a surge in freelance workers and goes so far as to call it "the industrial revolution of our time." Sara Horowitz, the series' author and founder of the nonprofit Freelancers Union, describes what she calls the "freelance economy," in which "over 42 million Americans are working independently—as freelancers, part-timers, consultants, contractors, and the self-employed." Horowitz goes on to argue:

> We haven't seen a shift in the workforce this significant in almost 100 years when we transitioned from an agricultural to an industrial economy. Now, employees are leaving the traditional workplace and opting to piece together a professional life on their own. As of 2005, one-third of our workforce participated in this "freelance economy." Data show that number has only increased over the past six years. Entrepreneurial activity in 2009 was at its highest level in 14 years, online freelance job postings skyrocketed in 2010, and companies are increasingly outsourcing work. While the economy has unwillingly pushed some people into independent work, many have chosen it because of greater flexibility that lets them skip the dreary office environment and focus on more personally fulfilling projects.

Because workers in this freelance sector of the economy are not employed by typical companies, Horowitz argues, they fall outside of many of the protections that were put in place by the New Deal, a legislative agenda that was driven through by Franklin Roosevelt as an implicit acknowledgment of the dramatic shift in work from the farm to the factory. These workers, whether solo practitioners or operating within small business, also do not have corporate human resources and training departments.

Given economic realities at the time I am writing this book, there is little indication that the situation will change for traditional employees, and there is every indication that the ranks of freelancers will grow. In their promotional efforts as well as in the types of content and learning experiences they offer, smart educational providers have a tremendous opportunity to find innovative ways to target and support one or both of these audiences.

FROM REMEDIAL EDUCATION TO LEARNING

The data concerning how well prepared young adults in the United States are as they exit our higher education systems and become prospects for the continuing education and professional development market are disturbing:

◆ A 2010 study by the Georgetown University Center on Education and the Workforce suggests that by 2018 the United States will need 22 million new college degrees—but will fall short of that number by at least 3 million postsecondary degrees, associate's or better. The shortage amounts to a deficit of 300,000 college graduates every year between 2008 and 2018.[4]

◆ In a recent survey of more than 400 employers, *only 23.9 percent*—that is, less than a quarter—reported that new job entrants with four-year college degrees have "excellent" basic knowledge and applied skills.

◆ In the same study, 43.4 percent of employers reported that the preparation of high school graduates was "deficient."

◆   Finally, another survey of 217 employers found that half the
companies provide readiness or remedial training, but most are not satisfied with the results.

The message from these examples and a range of other research is
clear: There is and will continue to be a lack of sufficiently educated people entering the U.S. economy in the foreseeable future. And this is happening at a time when the job market, as already noted in this chapter, is
shifting toward "high-talent" positions. If this fact alone does not suggest a major need and corresponding market for continuing education
and professional development, I don't know what does. Add to this the
data about the frequency with which people switch jobs—and potentially careers—and it is clear that we face both a significant challenge and
a significant opportunity.

Perhaps more worrisome than the issues we face with postsecondary
education, however, are the gaping cracks visible in our foundational
K–12 systems. At least since the passage of No Child Left Behind, the
relentless focus on standardized testing in our schools has diminished the
opportunity for teachers to expose students to a diverse, rich array of
content and contexts representative of the type of world into which they
will eventually emerge. As numerous critics of the U.S school system
have noted (I among them), this obsession with a misguided version of
"accountability" is resulting in students who have neither a sufficient
command of basic content nor the skill set required to be effective lifelong learners.

Testing aside, the traditional nature of school as an institution is
unlikely to produce individuals well equipped to function in the learning
economy. While there are notable exceptions, school as it currently
exists is based almost entirely upon a *dependency* paradigm. The vast
majority of work is structured for the student and delivered to the
learner with a much smaller amount being self-directed or at least collaborative. The proportions need to be flipped, or at least balanced. *Self-
directedness* is a key aptitude that the successful lifelong learner must
possess, but we are not cultivating this aptitude at a sufficient level.

Even to the extent that our traditional elementary and higher education institutions can, through their own efforts, align themselves more to the times, they will still only be a partial solution because such a large percentage of our learning needs arise in the forty-plus years that follow formal schooling. This is where self-directedness assumes a vital role, but also where there needs to be a rich network of learning and knowledge support that reflects the complex world in which we now live and work. Trade and professional associations are one existing part of this network; college and university continuing education departments are another. Organizations in each of these groups are struggling, to varying degrees, to keep up with rapidly changing needs and expectations. Associations, in particular, face the question of whether they remain relevant in a world where communities of interest can connect readily without them. Organizations need to rise to the new challenges of the lifelong learning marketplace—and there is plenty in this book to help them—but even assuming they do, demand is such that there still will be gaps to fill.

FIVE TECH TRANSFORMATIONS

Technology is a theme that runs throughout this book. As important as the other factors I discuss here may be, it is technology that has so far had the most visible, obvious impact on how we perceive learning and education. The fundamental shifts that have occurred in the global economy or that need to occur in our educational systems can be difficult to grasp, but smartphones, iPads, webinars, TED Talks (discussed in the next section), and degrees earned entirely online are relatively concrete, even if still amazing to many of us. We can point to ample evidence all around us, every day, that technology has made a difference in how we go about learning. And there is no reason to think it will stop.

From the perspective of the market for lifelong learning, I see five key areas in which technology has had, and will continue to have, a dramatic impact.

Access

There is no doubt that technology has dramatically expanded the range of tools and platforms available for delivering educational experiences, and by extension has blown open access to learning opportunities for the average person. The web, in particular, has all but eliminated time and distance—and, in many cases, cost—as barriers to learning, and made it possible for prospective learners to gain access to content and expertise that in the past would have required enrolling at a college or university, attending a conference, or spending a great deal of time in a library. Smartphones and other mobile devices continue to make access easier on a daily basis.

Education providers who continue to shrug off this phenomenon in the belief that educational experiences available over digital distribution channels are of inferior value do so at their own peril. The caliber and range of content, for starters, is truly astounding. With MIT in the lead, a global consortium of universities and colleges have long since (in Internet time) released major—and in many cases, *all*—parts of their curricula online for free and open access. This includes not just syllabi, but recorded lectures, readings, and all of the other supporting materials that go with classes at some of the world's top universities. The content is available through the universities' websites, but also through other popular, usually free distribution channels like YouTube and Apple's iTunes (which features an entire category called iTunes University).

Universities and other traditional education providers are not the only ones with access to digital distribution channels, and they are also not the only ones providing access to top experts. Less than a decade ago, for example, the annual Technology, Entertainment, and Design (TED) conference was an exclusive, high-priced membership event limited to an elite few with money to spare. Since the first release of recorded videos from the event in June 2006, it has become known to millions of users across the web and spawned additional business models, including the licensing of rights for local events under the brand TEDx. More recently,

TED has launched TED-Ed, a site that enables users to add collaborative tools, questions, and other resources to videos created by a select group of educators and animators (http://education.ted.com).

Subject matter experts of all types and all levels are now able to jump into the learning market, creating what I describe as the "Any Given Monday" phenomenon. Just as in the world of sports a seemingly outclassed team can rise to the occasion and beat a favored rival on any given Sunday, individual subject matter experts willing to put in the time and effort are taking their shot at nearly any area of learning you can name. On any given Monday you may open your in-box or scan industry news to find that a new thought leader — and learning leader — has emerged. For organizations like trade and professional associations that have traditionally dominated continuing education in their niches, this can be a particularly disturbing phenomenon. The subject matter experts on which these groups have relied for conference and seminar content can, and already do, compete with them directly more easily than has ever been the case before.

So, while one major outcome of the access to learning that technology provides is a larger and more vibrant education sector outside the traditional sector, the other is a much more competitive environment overall for anyone in the learning business. How to deal with this shift is a key topic in later parts of this book, particularly Chapter 3.

Involvement

While TED provides the ability for learners to comment on videos and potentially to become involved in events at the local level, its success has drawn primarily on the Internet as a *broadcast* medium. A critical extension of expanded access, though, is the scope and scale of *involvement* that technology has enabled. Learners do not have to be content with simply viewing or listening to content delivered over digital distribution channels. Using a variety of tools, ranging from simple chat to threaded discussion boards, multiway video (e.g., in which participants in a web-based video conference can see each other), and the whole universe of social media tools now available on the web, they can easily interact with subject matter experts and with other learners. What's more, they can easily become not only learners, but also teachers by actively contributing to the content and dialogue that comprise education experiences, or even by creating educational products to distribute to the world. YouTube, blogging platforms like WordPress, self-publishing platforms like Lulu and Amazon CreateSpace, and entrepreneurial learning marketplaces like MindBites—just to name a few out of thousands of potential examples—make it easy for anyone with expertise in a particular area to share that expertise with the world.

The possibilities for learner involvement and engagement can now scale to a degree that was previously unthinkable. In 2008, for example, two Canadian academics, George Siemens and Stephen Downes, launched the first ever "massively open online course," or MOOC, an experience that drew on tools ranging from blogs, wikis, e-mail, and an open-source learning management system to create a learning experience in which thousands of people from around the world participated. While Siemens and Downes helped to structure and facilitate the environment, the vast majority of the content was generated through participants blogging, tweeting, and leveraging a range of other social tools. All of this content was then connected by making use of the ability to tag—assigning a descriptive word or phrase to facilitate searching—and aggregate content on the web.

Large-scale learning is also happening in the context of massive, multiplayer games. The Institute for the Future, for example, has run a number of role-based "serious games" in which players tackle hefty issues like what life without oil would be like or how to prevent humanity from spiraling toward extinction. Thousands of people from around the world have participated in these experiences by imagining themselves within the scenarios engineered by the Institute and using a variety of tools to communicate with each other and contribute content. The group's latest game, *Catalysts for Change*, is set to launch as I am writing this book and will explore how to eliminate poverty globally. Jane McGonigal, the leader of the Institute's efforts with serious games, argues that game play on a large scale is one of the most effective mechanisms we have for broad societal learning and change.

Aside from providing for interesting new business models, these highly participatory approaches to learning will almost certainly create new learner expectations over time. To simply sit passively and attempt to absorb information will no longer be acceptable. At the same time, there are also implications for preparing learners properly. As I will note throughout the book, most of us are not well prepared by our experiences in school to be the types of motivated, self-directed learners who can take full advantage of these technology-fueled approaches to collaborative learning. This lack of preparation represents a challenge for learning providers, but also an opportunity for those who act to support learners well.

Chaos

The benefits of access and involvement do not come without a potential downside. There are more than 100 million blogs on the web at this point.[5] More than an hour of new video is uploaded to YouTube every minute, adding to the more than four billion videos that are viewed daily.[6] Smartphone usage in the United States passed the 100 million mark in early 2012[7], and the number of mobile "apps" is growing at a brisk rate daily. There is no accurate count of the number of online courses, webinars, and webcasts that flow through the Internet annually, but they no doubt measure in the millions at this point. For the prospective lifelong learner, the flow of information and choices becomes overwhelming quite rapidly.

A remarkable number of the "victors" in the Any Given Monday phenomenon are people or organizations (though usually with a particular individual leading the charge) who consistently and persistently help people make sense of the flow of information in a particular field, industry, or topical niche. They are there, week in and week out, often day in and day out, with a variety of content and perspectives. On the one hand, they contribute to the overwhelming flow of information, but they also play the important role of *curating* information—a topic I will return to in Chapter 7. They find and highlight the best of what is available, they repeat key themes and lessons, and in general, shape and lead thinking in their areas of focus.

As more and more people contribute to and share the vast quantities of digital content available through the Internet, it seems likely that the need for ways to filter and find focus will only grow. Better search technologies will certainly help to address this need, but actual human beings will also continue to play an important role. There is a significant opportunity in helping learners find their way through the chaos.

Diversity

An often-overlooked silver lining in the chaotic "cloud" of the Internet is the potential for embracing the diversity that it offers. In no previous time has it been possible for people to connect so rapidly, so easily, and so intimately across the globe—or even, for that matter, across town. We now have the opportunity to listen to, interact with, and learn from a much more diverse range of people and ideas than we might ever have encountered had we lived in other times. Since I started blogging in 2007 I have, as a direct result of my writing, connected to and communicated with people from Canada to Malaysia to Japan, and I have no doubt that doing so has enhanced my knowledge and understanding in a variety of areas.

Of course, the opposite can also be true. The web gives us the ability to easily find people and ideas with which we agree, and we often tend to gravitate toward the familiar. Over time, we may find ourselves living and learning in an echo chamber, in which only our own perspective is reflected. For providers of lifelong learning experiences, there is a great opportunity to create value by leveraging the diversity that technology enables and helping people connect with new perspectives.

Intelligence

Finally, there is little that we do in a connected world that is not traceable, whether on an individual level, in the aggregate, or both. While clearly this phenomenon has implications for privacy, it also means that we are able to much more easily track the path of learning and change. At the extremes, this newfound ability to capture and analyze data has led to movements like the "quantified self," in which people strive for self-knowledge through meticulously recording and tracking data points about their diet, sleep, exercise, and other activities day in and day out.

At a less ambitious level, it is possible for the average person to use free or low-cost tools like an RSS (Really Simple Syndication) reader (see Chapter 2) or HootSuite to aggregate streams of information from a variety of places, tag and filter it in a variety of ways, and even generate analytical reports on it. The possibilities for personal learning dashboards—pages, not unlike iGoogle or My Yahoo!, where it is possible to collect and organize a variety of resources—ranging from very simple to highly complex and sophisticated, are practically limitless. This ability supports the access already discussed, but also creates new opportunities for learners to be able organize, personalize, and learn from the endless flow of data on the web.

On the learning provider side of the equation, these same approaches make it possible to assess, monitor, and participate in markets for knowledge and learning in a way that has simply never been possible before, especially for individuals or small organizations. This shift impacts product strategy and planning. It impacts marketing. It impacts ongoing support. In the chapters that follow, I address each of these areas in detail and provide practical guidance on how to leverage them in your learning business.

MIND MATTERS

Through advances in neuroscience and psychology we have come to understand more about the human mind in the past three decades than we did during the entirety of human existence to that point. This new knowledge has powerful implications for how we learn and how we live productive, fulfilling lives. So far, most of the traditional organizations in the lifelong learning market have barely scratched the surface in bringing this new knowledge to bear on how they deliver products and services. The standard lecture model, for example, still prevails in nearly all of the educational programming offered by trade and professional associations, college continuing education programs, and training firms. For better or worse, the widespread availability of easy-to-use webinar and webcasting tools has made the lecture model pervasive on the web as well.

Lectures do still have a key role to play in adult educations, but what we have come to know about the human mind and, in particular, how adults learn, suggests that most lectures could be improved upon greatly and that lectures in general may be taking up more than their deserved share of the lifelong learning landscape. We know, for example, that:

- Adults have a "self-concept" of being responsible for their own decisions and along with this a need to be seen as self-directed in their learning efforts.[8] Most lectures create more of a dependency situation in which both the speaker and the learner expect the learner to listen passively.

- Our attention span for absorbing new ideas and concepts does not stretch much beyond ten minutes, yet the standard lecture runs fifty to seventy-five minutes.[9]

- We tend to absorb and retain information much better through active forms of learning that push us to draw on past experience, make connections, and apply what we are aiming to learn.

- People often learn fastest and most thoroughly when information is conveyed in relatively small quantities and then repeated at intervals over time.[10] A lecture is by its nature a very limited format for this approach.

- In many cases, social forms of learning are most powerful. We "construct" knowledge based on interaction with others in ways that we may be unable to do on our own.

In many cases, lectures can be improved upon to address these and other issues. In other cases, the lecture needs to be abandoned, or at least supplemented with other approaches.

An emphasis on how people learn is not just a matter of educational practice: I believe it will become fundamental to attracting and retaining customers for learning products. The volume of information and "junk" learning experiences available in the aftermath of the web explosion is simply overwhelming. While it may always be possible to hook people with shiny objects and deceptive promises, it will become increasingly hard to sustain and grow an educational business if you are not delivering clear returns on the learner's investment. Based on years of interviewing adult learners, it is clear to me that the average adult wants to walk out (or log out) of a lifelong learning experience having achieved a clear and actionable advance in her knowledge or skills. This often does not happen, or to the extent that it does, any gains by the learner evaporate in the coming days and weeks. Moreover, it is rare for organizations that offer lifelong learning opportunities to actually measure whether learning has happened and whether knowledge and skills have been retained.

It is impossible, of course, for any learning provider to control learning outcomes completely. Too much depends upon the learner and any number of variables that can impact or interfere with the learning experience. Nonetheless, we know enough now about how people learn, how to deliver effective learning experiences, and how to prepare learners to learn as well as possible that not achieving clear, sustainable outcomes is simply inexcusable. For serious producers, I believe the gap between current educational practices in lifelong learning and the outcomes that would be most valuable to learners and those who employ them represents a significant opportunity.

GENERATIONAL BOOKENDS

The final force might be seen as the one that makes the impact of the others inevitable. As generations grow older and new ones come of age in the midst of economic, educational, and technological shifts, expectations and needs are shifting as well.

While too many discussions of generational differences focus on aptitude ("younger people are simply better at technology") and attitude ("young people like technology more than older people do"), the more salient and accurate point is simply that younger generations do not think of technology as a distinct, special category of life.[11] Generations that have grown up with mobile and social technologies in a truly global economy simply have different expectations for how they will engage with the world and learn throughout their lives. With the range of options now available to them, these people are accustomed to simply checking out from whatever doesn't provide value and going elsewhere at the drop of a hat.

As I've written in *Shift Ed*, the ways that the upcoming generations "go about knowing the world may, in fact, position them to be some of the most effective learners that humanity has yet produced." Marc Prensky, originator of the term "digital native" and author of *Teaching Digital Natives: Partnering for Real Learning*, argues that:

> Ironically, it is the generation raised on the expectation of interactivity that is finally ripe for the skill-based and "doing-based" teaching methods that past experts have always suggested are best for learning, but that were largely rejected by the education establishment as being too hard to implement.[12]

While schools may be somewhat slow to address this shift, this does not mean that today's young people will not have different expectations as they enter adulthood. It seems reasonable to assume that Facebook, YouTube, Google, and the wide array of sophisticated games younger generations have been reared on will result in different behaviors and different expectations. We already have generations of adults who are bored with webinars and the typical seminar. That boredom will multiply many times over in the decades to come.

And there is, of course, the other end of the spectrum to consider. The retirement of the baby boomers marks a fundamental shift in what it means to be an older adult, at least in the developed world. There are now more people above the age of 60 than has ever been the case before, and members of this group are much healthier and much more active than were their peers in past generations. Many are interested in continuing to learn, and a growing body of research in recent years shows that we are, in fact, capable of learning new things late into life. For some, learning is focused on picking up skills for a second or third career. For others, it is about personal enrichment and exploring topics that there was no time for in earlier years. In either case, with more than seventy million baby boomers in the United States alone, this is a huge market.

THE SUM OF THE PARTS

Any one of the five forces would have an impact on the demand for life-long learning. Put them all together, and it is clear that this is a market already experiencing massive growth and poised for much more. It will not just be a bigger market; it will be a different market, one that is much more competitive and entrepreneurial than is currently the case, and much more driven by technology and by a better understanding of how human beings learn. Certainly traditional providers of education and training will play an important role, but the demand is larger than they can fill, and even they will need to learn new tools and approaches if they expect to thrive. In the remainder of this book, we'll take a detailed look at these tools and approaches.

NOTES

1. "The great mismatch," *Economist*, Special Report on the Future of Jobs, September 10–16, 2011, p. 4.
2. "Number of jobs held, labor market activity, and earnings growth among the youngest baby boomers: Results from a longitudinal survey," U.S. Department of Labor, Bureau of Statistics Press Release, June 27, 2008. Retrieved from www.bls.gov/news.release/pdf/nlsoy.pdf. (Retrieved January 10, 2012 , http://www.bls.gov/schedule/news_release/2008_sched.htm).
3. As quoted by Stowe Boyd: www.stoweboyd.com/post/10343503705/productivity-is-for-machines-if-you-can-measure.
4. A. P. Carnevale, N. Smith, and J. Strohl, *Help wanted: Projections of jobs and education requirements through 2018, Executive Sum-*

mary, Georgetown University Center on Education and the Workforce, Washington, DC, 2010, p. 1.

5. Gary M. Stern, "Keeping Track of the Ever-Proliferating Number of Blogs," Information Today, Inc., February 15, 2010, www.info today.com/linkup/lud021510-stern.shtml.

6. Source of statistics: www.youtube.com/t/press_statistics.

7. "ComScore Reports January 2012 U.S. Mobile Subscriber Market Share," Press Release, March 6, 2012, www.comscore.com/Press_ Events/Press_Releases/2012/3/comScore_Reports_January_2012_ U.S._Mobile_Subscriber_Market_Share.

8. Elwood F. Holton III, Malcolm Knowles, and Richard A. Swanson, *The adult learner: The definitive classic in adult education and human resource development* (Taylor & Francis, Kindle Edition), Chapter 4: A Theory of Adult Learning, "The Andragogical Model."

9. John Medina, *Brain rules: 12 principles for surviving and thriving at work, home, and school,* (Perseus Books Group, Kindle Edition).

10. "Spaced Learning," http://en.wikipedia.org/wiki/Spaced_learning.

11. Harrison Weber, "Study shows that kids, unlike adults, think technology is fundamentally human," *Insider,* January 18, 2012. http://thenextweb.com/insider/2012/01/18/study-shows-that -kids-unlike-adults-think-technology-is-fundamentally-human.

12. David Hook and Jeff Cobb, *Shift Ed: A call to action for transforming K–12 education* (Corwin, Thousand Oaks, CA: 2010).

13. Mark Prensky, *Teaching digital natives: Partnering for real learning* (Thousand Oaks, CA: Corwin 2010).

CHAPTER 2

FINDING AND UNDERSTANDING YOUR LIFELONG MARKET

ENOUGH BACKGROUND. It should be clear by this point that there is a significant opportunity for serving the market for lifelong learning in all its forms. In this chapter, we'll start discussing the practical, hands-on steps you need to take to capitalize on that market. Specifically, we'll look at assessing *your* market for lifelong learning. Readers who are just getting started with launching a lifelong learning business or taking an existing business online should find all parts of this chapter helpful. Veterans may want to skim some sections—particularly those dealing with finding your market—but I would strongly urge you to adopt a "beginner's mind" (to borrow a phrase from Zen Buddhism) and consider reading all sections with fresh eyes and no assumptions about your market. You may discover opportunities you had not previously seen.

◆　◆　◆　◆　◆　◆

One of the most essential concepts for any business in the market of lifelong learning is that it is truly *lifelong.* In other words, there is the potential to enter into a sustained, long-term relationship with learners who have perennial interest in a particular area of knowledge. As obvious as this point may sound, it is one that is routinely overlooked. Instead of engaging with customers in a way that builds increasing value over time, many learning providers focus on selling a particular seminar or conference or online course without articulating a broader story into which the learner fits. When the next seminar, or conference, or online course rolls around, that same learner has to be sold again, or a different customer has to be found. In a world in which it is harder and harder to get people's attention, much less inspire enough interest and desire to get them to pay for something, this is madness. To fully capitalize on the market for lifelong learning, you need to find a solid niche with needs that you can serve over time and then focus on delivering value and creating long-term, loyal relationships within that niche.

That's easy enough to say, but how do you do it?

As someone reading this book, you may already have many of the fundamentals in place. You (or your organization) most likely already possess expertise in certain areas, and you probably already have some idea about the general makeup of your market as well as the learning needs that exist in it. If you happen to be the type of person who would be a prospect for whatever you plan to offer, that's even better. You can tap your own needs and perspectives when thinking about how to really connect with long-term market needs. Whether or not you have this insider viewpoint, however, it is important not to make too many assumptions. You need to commit a bit of time and effort to making sure you really understand the market. Fortunately, this is one of the areas that have been truly revolutionized by advances in technology. While even relatively basic levels of market assessment used to require a significant investment of both time and money, a very rich assortment of assessment tools is now available at little or no cost. In this chapter we'll look at how these tools can be applied to a basic four-part process for market assessment:

1. Searching
2. Listening

3. Asking

4. Testing

Before we dive into the process, though, let's consider for a moment what sort of market you are trying to find.

WHO ARE YOUR POTENTIAL FANS?

Former *Wired* editor Kevin Kelly has suggested that anyone working as an artist these days can build a solid business based on cultivating a relatively small base of "true fans." For Kelly, an artist is pretty much anyone who is a producer or "maker," whether of music, painting, books, or any other form of intellectual property, and a true fan is "someone who will purchase anything and everything you produce."[1] He muses that to make a living, the average artist needs to acquire only 1,000 true fans.

This "true fan" concept serves as a useful rule of thumb for anyone debating whether to jump into the market for lifelong learning, but also for those who may be wrestling with how to take their current business into the future. Again, "lifelong" is the key term. Think of yourself as a new rock band aspiring to stardom. Selling a CD here or there is great, but what you really want are groupies. You want people who will download all the songs you post on the Internet. People who will show up whenever you perform and bring their friends. People who will spread the word. You aren't selling to these people just once. In fact, you often aren't *selling* to them at all. The vast majority of your interactions with them are not transactional in nature. They are about building a long-term relationship. And when your fans do buy something from you, you sell them more than just a product: You provide them an experience, a part in an ongoing story.

I know from my own experiences that the "true fan" concept is one that is not embraced frequently enough in the market for lifelong learning. In my work with trade and professional associations, for example, I find it is very common for members to participate in only one or two educational experiences a year, and in spite of sending in a check for membership, to really not be engaged with the organization in any meaningful way. These are not fans. These are simply customers who are on autopilot. For the short term, they provide revenue, but there is not a whole lot of reason to trust that they will be around for the long term. Similarly, I am the graduate of two institutions of higher learning, and most definitely have an interest in continuing to learn about the major topics I studied at both institutions. And yet, neither institution has made a noticeable attempt to engage me as a lifelong learner—only as a prospective donor.

In both of these cases, the opportunity to cultivate true fans is wasted. And, of course, the opportunities for others to step in are ripe. Don't make that mistake. As you consider your market, don't think in terms of transactions; think in terms of relationships. Do you see the potential for building a strong tribe? Kelly's "1,000" is only a proxy, of course: depending on the specifics of your business model, you may ultimately require a much larger or possibly a smaller customer base. Nonetheless, as a starting point, it is useful to ask the very concrete question "Does it seem reasonable that I can build strong relationships with 1,000 customers to whom I can provide consistent value over time?"

If you have an established customer or membership base, you may already have a sense of whether all or a significant enough segment of this base represents true fans, or at least potential true fans. In this case, you will want to turn to the techniques discussed later in this chapter to gauge demand. If you are starting from scratch, however, you need to spend some time thinking about, and perhaps doing a bit of research on, the size of your prospective market. For planning purposes, I'd recommend assuming that you will be able to sell to no more than 1 or 2 percent of your target audience. That means you should be looking for a total audience of 50,000 to 100,000 if you want to end up with 1,000 fans. In some cases, it may be obvious whether a market of this size exists. If you are targeting small-business owners, or lawyers, or nurses, for example, you can be certain, without doing any research, that the market is large. Even within these large markets, however, the slice that will value your products may be much smaller. Or you may have a more obscure market in mind in the first place; for example, people with a specific medical condition. While it may not be possible to find an exact number for the audience you have in mind, there are a number of free or low-cost resources that may help. These include the following:

- The Occupational Employment Statistics from the Bureau of Labor Statistics provides employment data on more than 800 different occupations.
  www.bls.gov/oes

- The Statistical Abstract from the U.S. Census Bureau provides a variety of data about different demographic groups in the United States.
  www.census.gov/compendia/statab

- The University of Texas Libraries site provides links to a long list of places to find demographic, occupational, and variety of other data globally.
  www.lib.utexas.edu/refsites/statistics.html

If by some chance you are not able to find numbers for your market through searching or using these resources, don't fret; the techniques described in the next section will help.

What Do You Know?

Before you engage in more formal research efforts, you should put significant effort not only into considering the potential size of your audience, but also into understanding the characteristics of audience members, and in particular, *the kinds of high-value, positive results they might be looking for that you could provide through training and education.* Use questions like the following to establish one or more profiles of the people you are trying to reach with your offerings:

- What are the key challenges and issues people in the target group are facing, and what do I already know—or think I know—about how they are dealing with these challenges and issues?

◆   What are some of the key characteristics or habits of these people? Are they highly educated? Do they tend to travel a great deal? Do they typically work very long hours?

◆   What are their key motivations and desires? Motivation plays a significant role in whether and how people are willing to invest their time and money in education. Ideally, you want to understand as much as possible about the *intrinsic* motivations of your audience, the type of motivation that comes from inside rather than from the promise of an external reward or punishment. In other words, what really makes them tick?

◆   What is the likely level of prior knowledge about the issues or topics that will be addressed in my offerings? This will be one of the biggest determinants of your learning strategy and may be a significant factor in the business model you select. How accomplished a person already is in a particular topic or skill impacts his or her ability to engage with new material. You don't want to deliver offerings that are too advanced to novices, or that are too basic to experts.

Unless you can point to a wealth of strong evidence, treat your answers to these types of questions as theories and assumptions, not as known facts. I often deal with organizations that are quick to stereotype their target audiences. For example, "Our customers are engineers, so they are introverts and aren't interested in collaborative learning experiences." Maybe this assessment has some validity, but it may also be the case that it is patently false or that it is true in some circumstances, but not in others. Acting on it without validating it can lead to a lot of wasted time and effort.

Finally, based on the profile you have developed, try to put yourself in your learners' shoes and engage in the very sorts of activities in which you expect them to engage. If, for example, you want to build a community where learners will actively contribute to the content and the conversation, what experience do you have with similar communities and what have you found to be valuable—or challenging—about them? Or, if you have never purchased an expensive online course, why are you expecting your learners to do so? You need to go through the process of experiencing what they might experience with your offerings.

BROAD STROKES WITH SEARCH

Once you have considered the potential size and nature of your audience, it's time to begin testing your theories and finding out more about the true behavior of the people you hope to serve. Throughout the sections that follow, I place a strong emphasis on behavior and observation rather than relying on direct input from prospective customers about needs and preferences. People are notoriously bad at predicting what they may need in the future, but you can draw some very useful conclusions from what they actually do in the present or have done in the recent past. A key place to look for initial clues about behavior in your market—and one that is often overlooked—is the search engines.

Search engines in general—and Google, in particular, given that it is by far the most popular search engine—provide an amazing trail of evidence generated by searchers' needs and desires. They also provide a lot of evidence about prospective competition. The key to capitalizing on this information is to put yourself as much as possible in the mindset of the profiles you developed in the last section. What are some likely words or phrases these people would type into a search engine if they were looking for something similar to what you have to offer? Start your research efforts by doing several broad Google searches based on those keywords and phrases.

If, for example, your focus is on helping small businesses with cash-flow issues, you might type in "small business cash flow." (Don't use any quotation marks or brackets around your search terms. These will narrow your results,

IMPORTANT TIP:

If you have a Google account, make sure you are logged out of it when you search. Google has moved increasingly toward providing personalized search results. You want to see what Google thinks is of interest to your market, not what is of interest to you.

and at this point, we want to see what the broad results are for your keywords.) When results come back on your search, there are three main points of information that will be of interest.[2]

1. What is the nature of the results? For general searching in Google, I find this to be by far the most helpful piece of information. Take a look at the types of results that come up in the first few pages, and particularly page one. How do they align with what you propose to offer? How well do they seem to align with the assumptions you have made about your market and the profiles you have established for your learners? Do they suggest needs that are similar to those you propose to serve? Do you see anything that might be direct competition or a substitute for what you want to offer? As you view the types of results that are coming up—including the ads that appear—you may want to adjust your search by removing words that don't really relate to the topic you have in mind. In the case of "small business cash flow," for example, a lot of results that have to do with getting loans or using specialized software come up. Assuming that I don't feel these are relevant to my product, I could remove at least some of these results by telling Google to ignore certain words. Just add any word to your search terms, but put a hyphen ("-") (which serves as a minus sign) in front of it. In this case, based on words that appear in some of the results I don't consider relevant, I might add the following: -loan -software -factoring -financing. As I do this, my results update in real time, and even the ads over at the right side of the page change.

2. Are there ads? Google's main source of revenue is the ads it sells to appear alongside search results. Look for a shaded box with text and links in it above your search results, and look over to the right side of the page for more text and links. These are paid ads, and their presence indicates that there may already be competitors. I say *may* because you also need to check the quality of the ads. Do they really relate to the search you did, or do they seem somewhat random? Google sells leftover space to larger advertisers, so it's possible you will see ads that are marginally or not at all related to the words you used for your search.

Believe it or not, the presence of relevant ads is a good sign: No one would buy ads if they didn't believe there was a market for whatever they were selling. While no ads does not necessarily mean no market, it is a warning sign that should be noted. On the other hand, a very large number of ads may indicate a very competitive market. Assuming you see some ads, scroll down to the bottom of the page and click "Next" as many times as it takes to get to a page with no ads. If it takes you a long time to get there (or you never get there), the market is likely very competitive. This happens to be the case with "small business cash flow." Don't fret, though; we are still at a broad level. There is likely to be significantly less competition as you narrow toward terms more closely descriptive of your proposed product.

3. Are there videos? While this may qualify simply as an extension of #1 in this list, videos are an important enough piece of evidence in training and education markets to merit special attention. Most videos that get uploaded to the web are either entertaining or instructional in nature. Google includes different types of content in the general search results it returns, so you may see video mixed in with standard web pages, e-commerce sites, and other types of results. If there are highly popular videos in the market, they will make it onto the top pages of the general search results, but you should also click on "Videos" in the left column of the search results to narrow your results to just videos. Ask the same questions about the nature and quality of these as you did about the general search results, and also take a look at what kind of comments the videos are getting.

Shaking the Trees

Don't confine yourself to just the initial broad search. Also narrow your search by attaching various "format" words to your niche keywords. For educational products, this would include terms such as:

- Seminar
- Workshop
- Conference
- Continuing education
- Training
- Webinar
- Video
- Book
- DVD

You may also want to include phrases that indicate a need or desire to learn. These might include:

- How to . . .
- Learn to . . .
- Be able to . . .
- Teach me to . . .

You will notice, if you try this specific example, that the number of search results that Google returns drops significantly with any of the format or learning needs words added to "small business cash flow," but there are still results, and these results are probably a lot closer to your actual competition. Pay attention to points #1 and #2 in the preceding section. Are there ads? What is the nature of the results that come up?

While you are engaged in the process of the search, also look in the left-hand column of the search results page and click "Related Searches." This will show you phrases people are searching on that are similar to the phrase you have been researching. It is often valuable to click on one or more of these and ask the same questions about the nature of the results and whether there are ads and videos related to the searches.

Note, too, that to run a series of searches takes no more than a few minutes. If your first couple of keyword phrases don't produce the kind of results you were hoping for, don't take that as a defeat but rather as an opportunity to brainstorm a bit about your topic. Always put yourself in the place of your prospective customer. What kind of value or outcomes would she potentially be seeking from your product? What new words can you try that relate to that outcome? In the case of a topic like "small business cash flow," often the real outcome a small-business owner is seeking is to reduce the stress of running a small business. So, searching on a phrase like "small business stress" might produce some useful results. (And, indeed, Google produces millions of results for that phrase at the time I am writing this book!)

Leveraging the Google Keywords Tool

To learn even more about potential demand and competition, take advantage of a tool that leverages the data that flows through Google's search engine and its AdWords platform: the Google AdWords Keyword Tool. If you don't already have a Google AdWords account, you can find the keywords tool at:

https://adwords.google.com/select/KeywordToolExternal

If you do have an account (recommended), the Keyword Tool can be accessed under Tools and Analysis.

While the Keyword Tool was designed primarily to help with developing a Google AdWords strategy, the data it generates are, by their nature, directly applicable to assessing markets. It would take a small book to dig deeply into effective use of the tool. To the extent you find it useful, I highly recommend *Google AdWords for Dummies, 3rd edition,* by Howie Jacobson, Kristie McDonald, and Joel McDonald. (See also the interview excerpt featuring Howie and Kristie later in this chapter.) For our purposes here, it is useful simply to run some of the same searches in the Keywords Tool that you ran in the Google search engine. What you will get back is a list of keywords related to your search along with some information about the search volume on those keywords and the level of competition for them—meaning the degree to which advertisers are competing with each other to have their ads show up whenever people search on those keywords. Don't take the numbers you see as gospel—it's not really in Google's interest to show you data that are complete and accurate. Rather, view this as a very rough gauge of the overall size and competitiveness of your market, and pay attention to the types of words and phrases that people are searching on. This will give you further insights about what's valued in the market and how you may want to position—or not position—your offerings.

Other Places to Search

While the various options Google offers will give you pretty solid high-level insights into the general market for your idea, two other places where you may want to do some quick searching are Amazon and SlideShare. A search on Amazon will tell you if books or other types of media have already been published in your general topic area—a good sign that there is demand—and also gives you the opportunity to read comments and review ratings, all of which can be helpful to you in gauging market needs. SlideShare (www.slideshare.net) is a site where people upload presentations on a wide range of topics. A significant percentage of these presentations come from people who speak or train on a particular topic. Again, the presence of items on SlideShare is an indicator of demand, and the slides themselves give you the opportunity to see how other providers are approaching your content area.

An additional search I would suggest at this point is for trade and professional associations that relate to your topic. Why? The presence of an association that is connected to your topic is a sure sign both that there is general interest in the topic—otherwise no one would go through the trouble to form and run a membership organization—and that there is likely a need for education related to the topic, given that one of the major focus areas of associations tends to be education. Even if—or perhaps *especially* if—you happen to represent an association that already serves a field related to your topic, this step is important to help gauge the number of other options your members may have. In the case of "manage small business," it is no surprise that there are many associations related to "small business." Perhaps somewhat surprising, however, is the fact that a search on "cash flow association" reveals that there is actually a cash-flow association as well as a range of other associations that address the topic of cash flow either directly or indirectly.

Finally, be sure to search both on whatever name you do business under, if you are already in the market, as well as on the names of any key competitors. You will want to know how and if you are showing up in the first few pages of search results and whether any unexpected results—for example, customers' complaints—show up. The same applies for your competition. How strong are their search results? Do you turn up any news or other information about them that might help you better understand your market? A little later in the book I'll cover making these sorts of searches part of an automated process, but for now, simply note any results that seem useful for assessing your overall opportunities and challenges.

TUNE IN AND LISTEN

Assessing your market with search is powerful for getting a high-level sense of potential market size, demand, and competition, but because search results don't provide contact with actual customers, the view they give into customers' real needs and desires is limited. By using social media tools like Twitter, LinkedIn, and Facebook in combination with search, you can find and "listen to" conversations that relate directly to your market and products. Doing this can help with assessing overall demand. It can also provide insight into specific market issues and needs and help you determine whether your theories and assumptions about the market are correct. Information gleaned from social network listening helps drive further assessment and, ultimately, product design. Additionally—and perhaps most important—by tuning in to social networks early, learning providers begin to build the relationships that will ultimately support successful promotion and distribution of their products.

Assembling a Dashboard

Listening in to market conversations is an ongoing process that starts during the assessment phase, but should remain active throughout the life of your business. One of the key initial steps is to create a dashboard to facilitate your efforts. While there are a number of good paid tools that you may want to investigate, a very good free option is to use an RSS reader like Google Reader as a platform for collecting multiple streams of information from the web into one place.

REALLY SIMPLE SYNDICATION

"RSS" stands for "Really Simple Syndication," a technology protocol that enables information to be packaged up and distributed around the web in an efficient and usable manner. I tend to think of it as being like the radio spectrum of the web, or perhaps more accurately, the ham radio spectrum. Traditional radio, because it is dependent upon large and expensive transmitters, is a one-to-many broadcast medium. Most people can receive a traditional radio broadcast, but they can't send out their own broadcast. Ham radio, on the other hand, relies on much less expensive equipment that hobbyists can afford. Ham radio operators receive broadcasts from other operators, but they also send out their own broadcasts.

RSS enables a similar dynamic on the Internet. Pretty much anyone can set up a blog, podcast, or other format that relies on RSS to send out content across the web, and anyone can make use of an RSS reader, podcast "catcher," or a variety of other methods to receive and manage broadcasts from others. Unlike ham radio, though, RSS is not relegated to less desirable parts of the Internet; it is available wherever the Internet is available. As a result, it is one of the key technologies that have democratized publishing on the web.

Google Reader was created as way to easily subscribe to and read blogs, and indeed this is one of the first ways in which you will want to use it. By going to Google's blog-specific search engine at www.google.com/blogsearch or simply by entering terms into the search box that appears when you click "Subscribe" in Google Reader, you can locate and subscribe to blogs that relate your market. By doing this, you can get a feel for what people who are writing in and about the market find important, and by reading comments on the blogs, you may get a much better feel for the types of customers you will be targeting. By submitting comments yourself, you can also begin to build up relationships with bloggers who eventually may be important allies in reaching your market.

Subscribing to blogs, however, is only one way to use Google Reader or any other RSS reader. You can also use it to keep a tab on searches you run through the Google Alert service, Twitter Search, and any other search service that offers the ability to subscribe to a feed. By doing this, you can get real-time or nearly real-time updates on conversations across the web that relate to your marketplace.

Google Alerts (www.google.com/alerts) is a good starting point for setting up some feeds related to your market. On the alerts search engine, you can enter your terms and then run a search that spans Google's networks, including its news sites, YouTube, and blogs. When you create an alert, you can set the "Deliver to:" option to "Feed," which will create an RSS feed that can then be added into Google Reader. As new items appear across Google's network, these will automatically flow into your feed. The types of items to search on in Google Alerts include some of the most important keyword phrases you used in your earlier search efforts as well the names of key competitors. In most cases, you will want to put these in quotation marks to ensure that Google returns only items that contain these exact words. Otherwise, you may end up with a lot of irrelevant junk in your feed stream. Note, too, that you can use all of the advanced features of the Google search results page (down the left side and also under the Options icon toward the top right) and then save these searches by scrolling to the bottom of the page and clicking "Create an email alert for [your search text]." By doing this, you can create some very targeted searches to track on a regular basis.

While standard Google searches are a key source for information, they may not readily surface relevant conversations happening across forums and social media sites. By tuning in to these, you may be able to discover how prospective customers are talking about the issues your educational options address. One option for doing this is to click "Discussions" in the left-hand column of the results for any Google search. This will produce results from forums and discussions indexed by Google (though seemingly with a strong preference for Google's own Google Groups). Another option is BoardReader (www.boardreader.com), which tracks a wide range of forums and discussion boards. In either case, you can save the search results as a feed to your dashboard.

Aside from discussion boards and forums, it is also possible to set up feeds from most (though not all) social networks. Doing so can become overwhelming pretty quickly, though, and some of the major sites like Twitter and Facebook don't make it particularly easy to do. Fortunately, there are a number of services out there that allow you to run a search across multiple channels at once. One example is Social Mention (www.socialmention.com), a site that allows you to run a single search across multiple media types—e.g., social networks, blog comments, images, and audio—and also select specific channels you want to include, such as Facebook, Twitter, LinkedIn, and so on. The results that are generated can then be subscribed to as an RSS feed so that they can be incorporated into your dashboard. Using a tool like this can save a great deal of time, and because it is usually possible to specify sources for the information you receive (for example, include Twitter, but not Facebook), you can tweak these searches over time as you determine which channels are providing the best information.

Tweaking the Dial

When you set up a range of searches through Google Alerts and social media sites, you will likely get some good initial information but then quickly feel overwhelmed by irrelevant or repetitive results. Don't despair: "Listening" can provide short-term insights, but it is primarily a long-term strategy. Glean whatever insights you can from your initial findings and then continue to adjust both your search terms and the channels you search over time. You will find that some search terms and channels simply need to be eliminated, while others can become much stronger with the addition of words that narrow their scope or of "operators" like minus signs to eliminate irrelevant results. Also, take advantage of the capabilities within Google Reader or whichever RSS reader you use to organize items into folders, tag items, and "star" items. These tools can help greatly when it comes to reviewing and using the information you have gathered.

I spoke with Dorie Clark, a marketing expert and author of Reinventing You: Define Your Brand, Imagine Your Future *(Harvard Business Review Press) about the power of listening. Here's what she had to say:*

In the past you would have had to pay thousands of dollars for focus groups or customer surveys or other approaches. Now you can get a lot of information simply by listening on online channels. It doesn't necessarily replace the other methods, but it supplements them in an important way, and depending on your budget, it's also a much more economical way of finding out what is on the minds of your customers.

As business owners or association leaders it's important for us to think about how peoples' expectations have risen. They do expect higher levels of responsiveness and customer service. But also it's a great way to reach out to people proactively and really surprise them. You can go above and beyond if you're following key people on Twitter and you see that they are writing about things related to your industry, related to your company, related to keywords that you're monitoring. Then you can reach out and "tap" them and say, "Hey, have you thought about . . . ," "Have you heard about this?" And that level of responsiveness, of feeling like you're really being listened to and heard, is pretty remarkable. It can build some serious brand loyalty.

Get the full interview with Dorie at www.learning-revolution.net/podcast/.

Going to the Source

While tracking saved searches can produce some great information, a next step for the conversations you locate is to click through to the original to get more detail and more fully follow the thread of the conversation. You should also spend some time going straight to the source to begin with, particularly on major networks like Facebook and LinkedIn, where not all conversations are accessible by outside search engines. Look for relevant groups of users on these networks (on Facebook, groups show up automatically in search results; on LinkedIn, you can set the search function to "Groups"). Also, search directly on major forum sites like Google Groups and Yahoo Groups as well as on question-and-answer sites like Quora.com and Ask.com. Within groups or discussion forums, you can often turn up relevant conversations by searching on phrases that indicate someone is looking for the solution to a problem. These might include:

- Can anyone . . .
- Has anyone . . .
- Looking for . . .
- Trying to find . . .
- Question about . . .
- Advice about . . .

Look for a frequently asked questions (FAQ) page on any group you search. What kinds of questions are being asked? Look also for "power" users—people who seem to be particularly active in discussions related to your area of expertise—and even competitors. You may want to connect with or follow these people.

Be sure, also, to explore some of the trade and professional associations you discovered in your earlier searching. Many times these organizations offer listservers and discussion forums as part of their membership benefits. Depending on the costs involved, it may be worth joining simply to be able to tap into these conversations and listen to what people in a particular field or industry are saying. If you happen to represent an organization that offers listservers or forums, make it a regular habit to review the conversations on them. You will often find clues that lead to new offerings, and occasionally you may even find a "slam dunk." The Florida Institute of CPAs, for example, identified a slam dunk by tuning in to a discussion about "comfort letters" on its federal tax listserver. (A "comfort letter" is a letter from an accounting firm assuring that a company is financially sound.) Ned Campbell, the senior director of education was paying attention, and when he noticed that an initial post about comfort letters quickly led to forty additional comments, he knew there was an opportunity. "Comfort letters are beyond the scope of what a CPA can typically provide for their tax clients," Campbell told me. "However, there is a tremendous pressure in the marketplace to provide these letters." Campbell and his team reached out to a subject matter expert (SME) to get input on the topic, and within five days of the first post had put together a two-hour webinar titled "Just Send the _____ a Letter! Webinar." Even with the Thanksgiving holiday looming, the webinar quickly generated ninety registrations from the thousand-member federal tax list. "Our members loved the topic, " said Campbell. "We provided them a service that was timely and relevant to their business needs, and it all came about from a single post on our member community."

While your listening activities may not often produce such immediate returns, this story illustrates how opportunities can be discovered— or missed—based on your listening habits.

When All Is Said and Done

The goal of all of this listening activity is not to drain your time away. Setting up a dashboard is one key way to ensure that you simply have to glance rapidly across a range of conversations to determine what, if anything, is of value. Conversations are valuable when they:

- ◆ Confirm—or refute—your theories and assumptions about customer needs

- ◆ Highlight new needs of which you may not have been aware

- ◆ Uncover competition you did not know existed, whether in the form of competing providers or in the form of new offerings from competitors you already knew about

- ◆ Surface potential allies, distribution channels, or other valuable relationships

By engaging in listening effectively and strategically, you should be able to gather a wealth of valuable insights into your market. These can then shape your additional efforts to assess your market.

TO LEARN MORE, ASK

Once you have clearly indentified your target market and focused in on the needs and issues most relevant to your prospects, the next logical step is to start asking some questions to get more detail about needs and to start testing your product ideas. There are a number of approaches to doing this, ranging from casual—like simply posting questions to one of the networks where you have been listening—to much more structured, like surveys or interviews. In all cases, the key to getting useful information from your prospects and customers is to ask the right types of questions.

A couple of important factors to keep in mind are that (1) people are notoriously bad about predicting what they will want or how they will behave in the future, and (2) it is very difficult to get people to accurately tell you *why* they do (or did) anything. Knowing these two limitations, it is tempting to drop the whole idea of asking the customers anything and simply plunge ahead. After all, Steve Jobs, who led Apple computer though a continuous stream of innovative new product releases, was famous for implying that customers simply do not know what they want. That is, it is up to you to figure it out for them.

While it is difficult not to agree to a certain extent, even Jobs was hardly operating in a vacuum. He watched and listened carefully to what was going on in the world around him, and he knew how to ask questions when he needed to. The key is to approach this type of market research not as if it is going to provide a crystal ball, but rather as a way to continue to form and test theories.

Posting to Networks

One of the key reasons to spend time listening on social websites, forums, listservers, and other network conversation areas on the web is that you can begin to develop a feel for the people and conversations in these places. You gain a sense of what to ask as well as where and how to ask it. These are particularly good places to explore open-ended questions and to find out how people have historically dealt with the types of issues your offerings are designed to address. If you have spent time listening on a network, as recommended, you will also have a sense of which participants are most active and what topics are of most interest to them. Whenever possible, it is valuable to enlist one or more of these people when you decide to post a key question. You may even connect with them directly first, to raise the question and see if it makes sense from their perspective. Additionally, ask if they will respond to the question once you post it to the broader community. The leadership of one or more active participants can go a long way toward ensuring that other group members will chime in. You may ask only one or two questions in a discussion forum or other network-based environment, but often you will want to go further and point people to a more comprehensive survey. In this case, it is also helpful to have a known and respected member of the network encourage others to participate in the survey.

Surveys

Based on existing market knowledge—including knowledge gathered through search and social networks—learning providers now have much more sophisticated abilities than they have ever had before to survey the market and ask specific questions. Tools like SurveyMonkey make it easy to develop and distribute web-based surveys, including not only authoring tools, but also preexisting question banks and options for offering incentives in a way that conforms to the array of states' laws.

Getting accurate, helpful input from your prospective customers can be challenging, but it is hardly impossible if you keep three key rules in mind:

1. The less sure you are about what people may want, the more you should lean toward open-ended, qualitative questions. Don't even assume that people need a "course" or other type of educational solution. Find out first what types of challenges they are encountering and what, if anything, they have tried to do to address these challenges. While qualitative questions are generally more time-intensive to analyze than are close-ended, quantitative questions, using them gives people the opportunity to tell you things you were not even looking for. Look for patterns—these can be used for follow-on surveys or interviews.

2. The less connection you have with your audience, the shorter your "ask" needs to be. The common wisdom is that surveys *always* need to be short. In my experience, this is not true. I've seen very high response rates on lengthy surveys, but these tend to be in situations where there is already a relatively tight relationship with the audience and participants see a clear connection between taking the survey and benefits they will receive in the future; for example, that they will be offered a better or wider range of education options. If you are venturing into new markets, though, be brief and to the point, and when possible, offer some form of incentive to encourage participation.

3. If you use multiple choice or other close-ended question types, focus more on identifying actions and behaviors rather than preferences

or predictions. While the past is not always an accurate predictor of the future, you can generally put more faith in what people have actually done than in what they say they will do. For example, to the extent I ask people about price in surveys, I ask them about what they have actually paid in the past for particular types of training experiences, rather than what they think a fair price to pay might be.

Interviews

You can use phone and in-person interviews to inform surveys or vice versa—there are arguments in either direction—but as a general rule, don't do them at the same time. The information from one is almost certain to help with the other. If you do not have good contact information for potential customers, you can use a survey as a way of creating a contact list. As one of your final questions, simply ask participants if they would be willing to participate in a follow-up interview, and if so, to provide a phone number and e-mail address. Use any key demographic data you collect as part of the survey—position, title, years of experience, etc.—to filter these responses and help you select the candidates you feel best represent your potential market.

In interviews, one of the areas I most like to explore is the challenges a person is currently encountering in work or other areas that relate to the potential educational offerings. What does he or she currently do to address these gaps, and how are those efforts working or falling short? Brief conversations along these lines with even as few as a dozen potential customers can tell you a tremendous amount about what your market needs.

TEST TO SUCCEED

With a firm idea of your audience and a strong working theory of what you will offer, it is now possible to test demand for your products more cost-effectively than has ever been the case before. By tapping into tools like paid search (e.g., Google AdWords), social networks, and e-mail lists (which smart learning providers will focus intently on building), you can run trial offers and "split test" multiple variations of product promotions with prospective customers. You can even go so far as to have them pre-purchase before a product is fully built. On a less formal note, simply by consistently offering targeted free content to your prospective audience—in the form of blog posts, newsletters, videos, and other formats—you can gauge interest, see what kind of feedback you receive, and shape your offerings accordingly.

Going through some version of a testing process, whether more or less formal, is absolutely central to successful business in the new learning landscape. As I related at the beginning of the book, it used to be quite common to invest large amounts of time and money into developing online courses and other offerings. Too often this level of investment was made, only to find out that the customers really didn't want the product—the classic "we built it but they didn't come" situation. Arguably, it was possible even in the "old days" to validate a product before launching into full-blown production and distribution, but these days, given the concepts already covered in this book, not validating your ideas just makes no sense.

A key concept that providers in the new learning landscape need to embrace is that of a "minimum viable product," or MVP. First introduced by Steven Blank in *The Four Steps to the Epiphany*, MVP has become a well-known term in the entrepreneurial community thanks to the success of *The Lean Start-Up*, by Eric Ries, one of the many entrepreneurs that Blank has mentored. The basic idea behind a minimum viable product is that you don't start by building a product with every feature you think your customers will want. Rather, you start with the most bare-bones offering that you think will meet customer needs, launch that into the market, and then move forward based on the feedback you receive. In some cases, this may mean no more than introducing an idea and seeing if enough prospective customers are willing to take action to express their interest. For learning providers, this may mean that you do not build a course, or organize a conference, or launch a membership learning site until a minimum number of people have committed to participating.

Entrepreneur Brian Clark, the CEO of Copyblogger Media, extends the idea of minimum viable product to encompass *minimum viable audience.* In the lead-up to launching a range of successful products— including the highly successful Teaching Sells membership learning community—Clark relied heavily on the responses and reactions he got to continually publishing content through his blog, Copyblogger. Additionally, when he launched the Teaching Sells learning community, it was far from a complete product. Rather, along with partner Tony Clark, he put together a basic platform and enough core content to make the community attractive to prospective members, and then continued to build it out over time as membership grew. As Clark puts it, through the ongoing interaction he and his team established with their audience, they were able "to make our MVPs more 'viable' from the start than we would have been able to otherwise. This led to better initial sales momentum, higher customer satisfaction, and ultimately more profit."[2]

The bottom line is that before you invest large amounts of time and money in building out new learning products, you want to see clear signs from your audience that the product will be a success. One key way to do this is by combining the search and listening processes I have already described with ongoing efforts to put content into the market, ask questions, observe, and then build to the needs that emerge. Even having gone through this effort, however, you should still consider formally testing the viability of new learning products by putting out an offer to which prospective customers can respond.

Establishing an Offer

To gauge interest effectively, you have to provide some way for your prospective customers to indicate by their actions that your offer has value (or, of course, doesn't). In the event that you already have some sort of established community, whether through an e-mail list, a discussion forum, a blog, or some other platform, that action may be as simple as replying to an e-mail or discussion post. For example, you may indicate that you will pull the trigger on offering a new seminar or webinar on a particular topic as soon as a certain number of people commit to attending at whatever price you name. I have witnessed Alan Weiss, well known as "The Million Dollar Consultant®," do this a number of times within his discussion community. He does not launch a new offering until enough people have committed to make it worth the effort. Indeed, Weiss even has a number of established items available in his online catalog that become available only once enough people have committed to a session.

Of course, it typically takes years of building up a community of followers before testing new offers in this way is viable, but even without an established tribe of followers, you can use a similar method as long as you can provide a sufficiently enticing offer. One way to do this is to create a "landing page" that provides key information and a way to take action. A landing page is simply a web page that is dedicated to a specific offer. Everything on the page—the words, the images, the flow of information—is designed to lead the visitor to take a specific action. Sometimes this action will be an actual purchase. In the testing stage, it usually makes sense for the action to be more along the lines of signing up for an e-mail list in exchange for access to something of value like an e-book or a video.

The following are the basic steps for successfully making use of a landing page. If you are not particularly skilled with technology, you may want to get some help with this, but keep in mind that a range of free and low-cost website tools like WordPress.com or Squarespace make most of this easy for even a novice to do reasonably well.

1. **Create an incentive.** These days, with time and attention being arguably more valuable than ever before, you have to have something of value to offer even to get someone to hand over an e-mail address. What tips, advice, or insights can you carve out from your offering and provide to those who might be interested? You can shape these into any number of forms, from a nicely formatted e-book to a string of brief white papers to one or more videos in which you cover some of your most valuable content. As a rule, don't hold back in the incentive. It's often tempting to feel like to best stuff needs to be protected and offered up only after a

check or credit card number has been handed over. But you will never get to that point if you can't make it clear up front that you have something of high value to offer.

2. **Create the landing page.** Your landing page is where you offer your incentive. You do this within the context of presenting your larger offer; in other words, what you are ultimately hoping the prospect will buy. While this page can be part of an existing website, it is better if it can be something completely separate, with no navigation links or other links on it other than those that relate to the prospect taking action.

3. **Provide for action.** Action can take a number of forms, from simply viewing a video to actually paying in advance for a forthcoming offering (with the usual incentive for this being a significant discount on the purchase price). In general, the action that I find most valuable at this stage is signing up for an e-mail list. People are usually not eager to hand over their e-mail addresses in our information-overloaded and spam-afflicted world, so while an e-mail address may not equal a purchase, it does usually represent a significant level of interest on the part of the prospect. Moreover, in signing up for an e-mail list—as opposed to just watching a video or downloading a document without having to sign up first—the prospect gives you both the means and permission for future contact. When your aim is to actually sell a specific product, as opposed to gain broader exposure for your brand, it is critical to know you can secure at least this level of commitment from a prospect. If you can't, the chances of the prospect actually paying for something from you in the future are slim.

Setting up an e-mail list is quite easy these days. Services like MailChimp offer free lists up to a certain number of subscribers (2,000 as of this writing). Other services like AWeber and Constant Contact start at around $20 per month. All of these services provide easy ways to generate a sign-up form and insert it into a web page. Just as important, they provide automated ways for users to confirm their subscriptions and to automatically send out a variety of follow-up e-mails to subscribers. Whatever you do, be sure to go with an established e-mail provider and *do* require subscribers to confirm their subscriptions. These precautions will help ensure that you do not get labeled as a spammer and that your e-mails actually make it to the inboxes of your subscribers.

I discuss more advanced landing page concepts in Chapter 8, but with even these basic concepts you have what you need to run a simple test.

A Down and Dirty AdWords Primer

Of course, it doesn't much matter that you have a test offer set up if you can't actually find anybody to view the offer. If you have been doing your foundational work of listening in on social networks and other communities and have started engaging on those communities, you may already be in a position to carefully post messages that point people to your offer. I say "carefully" because you definitely do not want to start selling before you have established yourself as a trustworthy member of a community. Additionally, if you have a website or blog that already attracts substantial traffic, you can use this as a tool for directing prospects to your offer.

Even if you can leverage social networks or your website, though, you may need to reach a bigger or different prospect base. And, of course, if you are starting pretty much from scratch—no website, no significant network connections—it may seem like there is little you can do to channel people to a test offer. In these situations, Google's AdWords platform can be of tremendous value.

Google created its AdWords program—the major source of the company's revenue—as a way for advertisers to create ads that appear only when someone is searching on words that are related to the ad. The advertiser then pays, in most cases, only if the searcher then clicks on the ad. The system has a few simple but brilliant advantages over traditional advertising. First, viewers of search results are subjected only to ads that may actually be of some relevance to them, so advertisers aren't wasting so much money on what have been called "spray and pray" approaches. Second, because advertisers usually pay only if a viewer clicks on an ad, they can be reasonably sure that they are paying for leads with a clear interest in whatever they are selling. Finally, all of this is readily measurable through tools freely provided by Google: You can see how often your ads appear, where they are positioned relative to other ads, and how many clicks you get. With just a bit of additional work, you can even determine whether these clicks ultimately convert into sales.

Naturally, all of this is extremely valuable from the standpoint of selling advertising, but what tends to be overlooked is that it is at least as valuable from the standpoint of assessing and testing markets. As we have already covered, the data gathered from AdWords can be used to gauge demand and competition in a market. But once you have a solid idea of what you plan to sell and to which markets, you can also create ads to test your idea. As Howie Jacobson, a leading AdWords expert and coauthor of Google *AdWords for Dummies*, 3rd edition, puts it,

> AdWords is actually a cheap and highly reliable wind tunnel you can rent by the click to discover and validate your market, test your messages and positioning, and increase your conversion rates and profits.
>
> Tests that took four months and half a million dollars in 1990 can be completed today in seven days for $350. The beauty is, everything you discover in these micro-tests can be applied in other media, including expensive and really-hard-to-test offline media like TV, radio, newspapers, event sponsorships, and billboards.[3]

Jacobson contends—and I wholeheartedly agree—that "to this day, Google doesn't fully understand what it's created."

To run an AdWords campaign, you need to first have a Google account. This can be set up free at www.google.com/adwords. Google provides good guidance on how to configure a campaign, but here are the basic steps to get you started:

1. Before even setting up the campaign, determine the keyword phrases that will be the basis for the campaign. Your aim is to test out your best guesses on what prospective customers might type in that

would lead them to your landing page. What problem are they trying to solve? How do they tend to talk about that problem? The work you have done so far should give you good insights into the language to use. Ideally, use keyword phrases that are two or three words in length. Doing this will help strike a balance between searches that are too general, which may attract unwanted traffic to your landing page, and ones that are too narrow, resulting in little, if any, traffic.

2. Name the campaign and define basic settings like the geographical area in which you want your ads to appear and the amount you are willing to spend per day on your campaign. (Once you have tapped out this budget, Google will stop running your ads for that day, but will start them back up again on the following day.) Under "Networks," select "Let Me Choose" and uncheck "Display"—for now you want to concentrate only on people who are actively searching for your keywords.

3. Create an ad group, including the first ad, and put in keywords for the ads in this ad group. Your keywords should relate directly to the text on your landing page, and keywords within your ad group should also be similar to each other. Don't, for example, group "marketing strategy" and "financial strategy" together. While these may be tied together by a focus on "strategy," the audience and the landing page content for them may be quite different.

4. For the ad itself, think in terms similar to those already covered for landing pages. Really, an AdWord ad is like a very concise, miniature landing page. You need to grab attention with a compelling, relevant headline (the first line of your ad), and then briefly convey key benefits and provide a call to action. Be sure, also, to include at least one of the keywords from the ad group in your ad text. The ad should relate very tightly to what you will actually offer on your landing page. Your goal is to attract clicks only from people who are highly likely to be interested in your landing page offering.

5. Create additional ads. Aside from testing your landing page, AdWords gives you the ability to see what works best for attracting people to your landing page. Run at least two ads initially to see which

performs better. Once you have determined the higher-performing ad, pause the lower-performing one and try another variation. Repeat this process until you have a feel for what language works best for driving clicks to your landing page.

6. Once your first ad is saved, your campaign is automatically live until you pause it. It will take up to a day for initial results to appear in Google, but once they do, track them long enough to see if you are getting click-throughs and if these are resulting in conversions on your landing page. If, after a few days, you are not getting a significant number of clicks, you may want to try new ad variations, new keywords (Google provides a keyword suggestion tool within AdWords), or potentially raise the amount you are willing to pay per click for your keywords. (Google also provides you with information on how high your bid needs to be to get you onto page one of the search results.)

7. If you are getting clicks, but no conversions, make one or two significant adjustments to your landing page to see how this impacts results. This may mean adjusting your headline or adjusting your offer—including, potentially, changing the price if a purchase is involved. Additionally, you may need to "throttle back" your visibility in search engine results by placing your keyword phrases in quotes (what Google calls a "phrase match") or brackets (what Google calls an [exact match]). In the case of a phrase match, your ads will show up only for searches that contain your keyword phrase plus any words included before or after it. In the case of an exact match, your ads show up only when your exact keyword phrase, with no other words included, is submitted by a searcher.

Unlike running a true advertising campaign, this kind of testing is done within a fairly limited time frame. Per-click costs can rack up pretty quickly. You don't want to empty your wallet in the testing process, and in any case, the strength of an idea should become evident pretty quickly. If ultimately you are managing to get clicks but do not seem to be able to get any conversions, you have a sign that you simply need to head back to the drawing board to rethink things. While this may seem discouraging, remember that it beats the heck out of blowing a lot of money on a product only to find out too late that there is little or no demand for it.

FINDING YOUR DOROTHY BOYD

What if you are a solo learning provider, or work at an organization that is strapped for time and money? How can you best make use of a pay-per-click (PPC) tool like AdWords to ensure you get worthwhile results? I posed this question to Kristie McDonald and Howie Jacobson, two of the coauthors of *Google AdWords for Dummies* and founders of Vitruvian Way, a marketing agency that specializes in the use of AdWords. Here's what they had to say.

Kristie:
When somebody doesn't have a lot of budget to work with, and they're looking to run a PPC campaign that is small and tight, what we tell them to do is analyze their market for their bull's-eye. What are the bull's-eye terms in your market—the terms that, if somebody types them in, their intent absolutely is to buy what you have? They are looking for you. They are looking for what you have.

For example, if somebody is looking to be certified by the Project Management Institute, and they type in "PMI Online Courses," they're clearly looking for *you* if you sell PMI courses. And you need to be there when they're looking, because otherwise your competitors will get them instead. If you have a small budget, you just need to look at your core terms. Don't try to experiment with other ones. Just use the core ones. What would somebody ask for if they were looking exactly for me? Then run that campaign.

Howie:
One of the functions of AdWords, or any sort of pay-per-click, is to test the rest of your sales funnel. It may be that AdWords is not the place where you're going to "kill it." There may not be a lot of traffic, or people may not be searching for it. It may be an impulse buy or

your competition has a business model that just makes it too expensive for you to advertise successfully for long.

But if you have an online business these days, the website is the nexus for whether people end up interested in you or not. And that's how I would initially use PPC—to do what Kristie says. To figure out, "Who's my bull's-eye?" Who are the people that I call the "Dorothy Boyd prospects"? Remember? That was Renée Zellweger's character in *Jerry Maguire*—the one he "had at hello." With your Dorothy Boyd prospects, you say "This is what I do," and they say, "That's exactly what I want." If you can't sell to those people, why bother with anybody else?

Get the full interview with Howie and Kristie at www.learning -revolution.net/podcast/.

A WORD OF CAUTION

It's always tempting to think that if we do enough research, talk to enough people, and are as thoughtful as possible in laying out our plans, there's no way we can miss. My view is that good assessment and testing can increase your chances for success, and at a minimum, it will teach you a great deal about your market that is likely to be useful over time. Don't be blinded by data, though, or get fooled into thinking you have it all figured out. People are complex, and markets full of people are even more complex. As science writer Jonah Lehrer says, in explaining about how scientific research often does not lead to the expected results,

> We live in a world in which everything is knotted together, an impregnable tangle of causes and effects. Even when a system is dissected into its basic parts, those parts are still influenced by a whirligig of forces we can't understand or haven't considered or don't think matter. Hamlet was right: There really are more things in heaven and Earth than are dreamt of in our philosophy.[4]

Like any other business venture, jumping into the world of lifelong learning involves risk. Do your research, make reasonable plans, but in the end, be prepared simply to make the leap and then respond rapidly to what you learn along the way.

NOTES

1. Kevin Kelly, "1,000 true fans," *Techium*, March 2008, www.kk.org/thetechnium/archives/2008/03/1000_true_fans.php.

2. Jacobson, McDonald, and McDonald advocate a simpler three-pronged approach in Chapter 4 of *Google Adwords for Dummies*, 3/e.

3. Brian Clark, "Five ways a minimum viable audience helps you create a successful startup," http://entreproducer.com/minimum-viable-audience.

4. Howie Jacobson, "How to test your advertising quickly, cheaply, and effectively," HBR Blog Network, *Harvard Business Review*, October 4, 2011, http://blogs.hbr.org/cs/2011/10/the_fastest_cheapest_best_eway.html.

5. Jonah Lehrer, "Trials and errors: Why science is failing us," *Wired*, January 2012, p. 109.

CHAPTER 3

BUSINESS MODELS FOR THE NEW LEARNING LANDSCAPE

IDENTIFYING YOUR PROSPECTIVE CUSTOMERS and understanding, as well as possible, how to deliver value to them is essential, but this is, of course, only the first step. Determining your approach to delivering products or services that maximize the value both you and your customers receive is the next step. This is your *business model.*

While most discussions of business models tend to focus on the point at which a revenue transaction occurs, there are really four important components to a successful model:

1. The **value proposition** to the buyer
2. The **resources** required to deliver on the value proposition
3. The options for generating enough **revenue** to cover resources
4. The **sustainability** of the model in the face of competition and other outside forces

Each of these has been disrupted in significant ways over the past several years as technology has evolved and learner expectations have changed along with it. *Convenience* and *relevance*, for example, have now become much more central to the value proposition of educational products and services than they have ever been before. This shift is a direct result of the dramatic increase in access that technology has provided. Customers have come to expect options that do not require travel and that can be accessed according to their own schedule. Business models *must* account for these expectations, whether that means maximizing convenience, emphasizing factors that add value beyond convenience, or taking a contrarian approach and making a lack of convenience a source of heightened value perception. Traveling to and paying for a TED conference, for example, can hardly be called convenient, yet demand is high. At the same time, generic one-size-fits-all training courses are becoming a harder sell because customers can now search the global catalog of the web for options that better fit their actual needs.

From the standpoint of resourcing, the combination of rapid change and lower barriers to entry means that *velocity* and *brand* have become much more important to resourcing than ever before. Velocity means more than simply moving quickly, as important as that is; rather, it is the combination of speed and direction. Producers today must know how to find resources quickly, move forward rapidly with those resources, and keep moving, preferably at an accelerating rate. As a result, it increasingly makes sense to "build the plane as you fly," ship a product that is good enough, and in general, to simply *do something* rather than to take years to strive for perfection. There may still be benefits to raising large amounts of capital and investing it in extensive research and development, but increasingly these steps come after an initial model has been proved. More and more they also come after you have built an audience for your offering, which requires getting attention, establishing authority, and cultivating trust: in short, building a strong brand.

Next, traditional revenue options, while they do still work, are getting more difficult. The time-honored way to make money from training and education is to build a course or other learning experience and charge a fee for it. Alternatively, you could seek some form of sponsorship (in some instances including grants or advertising), either as a supplement or replacement for direct revenue. Over time, you may create multiple offerings and collect them into a catalog. We can expect this scenario to become increasingly difficult if only because of the proliferation of options for both customers and sponsors. With so much content now available free or at very low cost, providers will find increasing opportunities to charge for some form of *validation*—for example, by awarding a certificate or other valued credential. Additionally, there will be growing opportunities for charging for higher levels of *intimacy* and *customization*. An example here would be giving customers direct, real-time access to an actual expert rather than the generic access that may be available at little or no cost on the web. Sponsors, on the other hand, will increasingly be looking for value other than exposure alone whenever they underwrite a learning experience. The ability to provide access to different types of *analytics*—related to demographics, behavior, and performance—will be an increasingly important driver of revenue going forward. Think, for example, of how Google and Facebook make their money. On the surface, it is from advertising. But what makes it possible to sell those ads in the first place is the very fine-tuned ad placements these companies can offer based on the treasure trove of demographic data they have collected from you and me.

Finally, the agility required to balance these factors in a marketplace that continues to evolve daily makes long-term sustainability a particular challenge. As I will stress in the next chapter, one of the key skills providers must cultivate in the new learning landscape is an ability to *position* themselves effectively and *differentiate* their offerings.

Add up all of these changes and many others and it becomes clear that more dynamic and innovative approaches to developing, marketing, and selling education are needed than many traditional learning providers have embraced so far. In the remainder of this chapter, I explore four business models for lifelong learning that take into account some combination of the changes I've just highlighted. Some of these are already proven models; some are more emergent at this point. Each, however, illustrates both significant opportunities and the challenges of doing business in the new learning landscape.

THE P² COMMUNITY MODEL

A while back I ran into a learning issue that, years before, would have gone largely unresolved. Namely, I had become intrigued with blogging, and having been at it for a year or so, was finding that it was starting to be quite valuable as a tool for building my own brand and growing my business. I was struggling, however, with how to build a bigger subscriber base and, in general, generate more business value out of my efforts. I had read books, and I tracked the efforts of a number of other bloggers, particularly people like Darren Rowse, who had already built quite a following on ProBlogger, a blog he wrote specifically to help people grow their blogs as businesses. Even so, there was nothing that provided quite the level of guidance and ongoing support that I felt I needed. Then the A-List Blogging Bootcamp (www.alistbloggingbootcamps.com/) came along.

Like many bloggers back in 2009—and today—I was familiar with Leo Babauta's blog Zen Habits. At that time, Leo already had well over 50,000 subscribers, and with the A-List Blogging Bootcamp, he was offering to share how he had seemingly come from nowhere to become a web publishing powerhouse. I was among the first to sign up for the bootcamp, and then among the charter members of the A-List Blogger Club launched by Babauta and his partner Mary Jaksch—the source of the idea for both the bootcamp and the club—as an ongoing training community for bloggers. I remain a member to this day, nearly three years later.

What the initial bootcamp and then the club provided was something I had really not experienced before in my professional development efforts, at least not in such a well-defined and focused way. It was an online course with a rich collection of videos, how-to articles, and other resources, but it was also very clearly a community. There were discussion forums that people actually used, and on which both Leo and Mary were active. And there were frequent real-time learning sessions using tools like the free Ustream video streaming platform. Most important, there was sense of enthusiasm that pervaded the community. The participants wanted to be there and were dedicated to getting something out of the experience.

All of this, it should be noted, was built on mostly open-source software. The WordPress blogging platform formed—and still forms—the core of the site. Leo and Mary used a low-cost plug-in to turn it into a membership site, and another add-on to create the discussion boards. E-commerce transactions for the original bootcamp as well as for monthly subscription fees for the ongoing membership were handled by a simple PayPal setup. The original bootcamp fee was a few hundred dollars, and the monthly membership is twenty dollars—adding up to an annual cost that is less than what it costs to attend most conferences. I should also note that neither Leo nor Mary were e-learning professionals or even professional trainers. They structured the content for the site and focused their facilitation efforts around the idea of being—as Mary put it—"insanely useful." It worked, and the A-List Blogger Club thrives to this day.

I asked Leo Babauta, cofounder of the A-List Blogger Club, about the effectiveness of online learning communities and whether he feels some people are better suited to them than others.

I'm not sure if it's limited to any particular type. I think most people do better with that than just reading some articles on a blog or a book. Books, I think, are amazing tools for learning, but again most of us will read something and maybe mark some notes to do something but not really do it. But when you have a community of people who are going through the change together, that's almost always going to be much more effective because you have the social element. We're all social animals, and when you see other people doing it and you are part of this community, you want to look good in that community. And so you do what you can to show that "yes, I can do it, too. I can do it along with everyone else."

You're also inspired by the other people going through those changes. You help each other out. So, I've always found it to be much more effective for almost anybody. There are some people who will pay for it and not really do it. But compared to books or blogs or even watching videos, a more hands-on community-oriented approach has always been more effective for pretty much any audience.

Get the full interview with Leo at www.learning-revolution.net/podcast/.

Where It Works

Broadly speaking, an approach like the A-List Blogger Club can work in any niche where core skills and knowledge are constantly changing or evolving. This description certainly applies to blogging, but it also applies to countless other areas of business and professional life as well as in more personal areas like health. Additionally, the approach applies well in areas of perennial interest where people can never really know enough. Just about anything related to running a small business, for example, might fall in this camp. On a more personal level, hobbies and avocations like gardening, fitness, and gaming are just a few examples from the inexhaustible list of areas in which large groups of people feel both purpose and passion.

Because there are so many areas in which this model can apply, where it works is really less important than what makes it work. Having participated in and observed a number of similar communities, I've found that they require two key elements truly to be successful: **purpose** and **passion**. The two of these working together have an exponential impact on learning. It is for this reason that I call these types of communities P^2—*Purpose* $\times$ *Passion*—Learning Communities. While common interests or occupations may be enough to spark some participation in a community initially, there have to be clear, focused outcomes that participants expect to achieve from participation. These may be highly concrete, like earning some sort of credential, or they may be somewhat fuzzier, like continually finding ways to grow your blog—but they have to be there, and the community as a whole has to sense that the purpose is being served. To this end, I've noticed that successful communities tend to have what is essentially a syllabus or curriculum at their core. The A-List Blogging Bootcamp and the A-List Blogger Club are structured around a series of modules, each of which contains multiple lessons

- ◆ 001 Kickstart Your Blog
- ◆ 002 Create a Blog That Rocks
- ◆ 003 Blog Growth Mastery
- ◆ 004 The Art of Blog Seduction
- ◆ 005 Write Like an A-List Blogger
- ◆ 006 Make Your Blog Pay the Bills
- ◆ 007 Create Courses That Sell
- ◆ 008 Ebook Mastery
- ◆ 009 Blog Video Mastery

These provide substantive content as well as points of reference from which much of the discussion on the site flows. In other words, Babauta and Jaksch didn't just throw some community tools into a website and hope meaningful learning would follow.

Consultant Alan Weiss, who has built a strong international brand as "The Million Dollar Consultant®" hosts a vibrant learning community in Alan's Forums (www.alansforums.com). While the community does not have the same sort of explicit curriculum found in the A-List Blogger Club, it is implicitly structured around the core concepts that Weiss has written about and taught for years. I asked Weiss about what makes communities successful, and in his answers, he draws an analogy with the Apple "app" community:

I think a true community, such as I have with Alan's Forums, is one where people interact. They're drawn together by the quality of the people there. They act as peers. They help each other, and in helping each other they help the overall profession. It's not dissimilar, by analogy, to the iPhone and apps. The more apps that are created, the more the people buy them, the more people are attracted, the more apps are created. Apple then creates an even better iPhone and the cycle repeats itself. So, that's what I mean by community. Not anyone can create a community. You have to have a strong brand, thought leadership, and intellectual property. And so, in boutique consulting, I've been able to do that.

Get the full interview with Alan Weiss at www.learning -revolution.net/podcast/.

The other part of the equation is passion. While not everyone will participate in a P^2 Community all or even most of the time, something like the classic 80/20 rule needs to apply: There needs to be a core 20 percent at any given time that really cares about the focus of the community and contributes to it regularly. As a general rule, the facilitator (or facilitators) of the community needs to be part of the 20 percent. In the case of the A-List Blogger community, the level of passion and participation was one of the factors that struck me right out of the gate. Over time, the interplay between passion and purpose have sustained and driven the growth of the community.

For organizations that are already based on a membership model in which education is only part of the focus, the P^2 Community model may, paradoxically, be challenging to make work. Most of these organizations, in my experience, try to be so many things to so many people that putting together a single community encompassing the entire membership dilutes purpose and passion to such a degree that the community never really takes off. Often, however, there are significant opportunities for focused learning communities within a broader membership base. The American Chemical Society (ACS), for example, is pursuing this approach with its recently launched Sci-Mind™ initiative (http://sci-mind.org). In many ways similar to the model used for A-List Blogging, Sci-Mind blends self-paced learning content with access to expert guidance and peer-to-peer learning using a variety of social media and collaboration tools. ACS has even taken things a step further by having learners complete an "Analyst" tool up front that helps them tailor the on-demand content they will cover during the experience. Learners then participate in a six-week "cohort" learning experience followed by ongoing access to the Sci-Mind learning community. ACS charges $1,495 to participate in a cohort. Having completed its first, it has three more scheduled for 2012. (For an interview with Jeff Standish and Stephanie Rizk of ACS, visit www.learning-revolution.net/podcast.)

Dave Will, chief executive peach of Peach New Media, is bullish about learning experiences similar to the one that ACS is offering through Sci-Mind. In collaboration with Higher Logic, a social media platform company, Peach has launched a Virtual Study Group offering that brings peer learners together for an intensive, focused learning effort over an extended period of time. Will told me,

> We brought three things together. We brought on-demand content; things for people to review and study on their own at their own leisure. We brought together a community, which allowed people to interact with each other, get to know the other people studying this topic, get into discussion groups about it, read some blogs from a subject matter expert focused on this particular piece of content. And then third, we brought in live discussions. Live discussions can happen online, they can happen over the telephone, they can happen with video cameras up, or it can be in the form of a webinar. However you want to do that is fine, but the idea is that it's a live discussion to process thoughts around what has been going on in the community and to process thoughts about what's been going on with the on-demand content. (Get the full interview with Dave Will at www.learning-revolution.net/podcast/.)

The Virtual Study Groups are generally paid offerings, and Will reports that a number of association clients are generating significant levels of income from them.

Downsides and Upsides

Successful P^2 Communities can be time-intensive to start and they require significant care and feeding over the long haul. In other words, you can't simply build it and expect them to come, much less stay. If you pursue this model, you have to be prepared to provide a continuous stream of content over time and to dedicate ongoing time to participating in and facilitating the community. Your goal is to create a sort of "flywheel" effect, in which the momentum you create within the community begins to build on itself. Getting to this point, however, requires significant effort.

You need to be prepared to assemble a relatively structured, content-rich site up front to drive participation and engagement in a P^2 Community. The level of thought and effort required to do this is often the main obstacle to creating this kind of community, but generally most organizations or individuals who have worked in a particular area of expertise for any period of time have more content to work with than they realize. The effort is more one of gathering and organizing rather than creating from scratch.

Certainly it helps to already have a large audience in place when you launch a community. Leo Babauta had this in spades, and many membership associations have an installed base as an inherent advantage. Even so, a P^2 Community does not have to be large to generate significant value and income. By combining "insanely useful" content with the marketing approaches described later in this book, even a newcomer can attract an initial base of customers that can grow over time.

The opportunity to grow and evolve over time is one of the main upsides to the P^2 Community model. This growth and evolution applies not only to participants in the community, but also to the content of the community. P^2 Communities can start with a relatively small amount of core content and then add more over time as member needs become clearer. A natural outcome of the ongoing interaction with and among customers is that it tends to surface new needs and thus serves as a sort of built-in market intelligence system. Based on this intelligence, you can add new core content to the community or even create paid spin-offs or premium content. A community may, in fact, be a better approach than the standard catalog for housing a listing of additional paid offerings. And, of course, members of communities themselves contribute a great deal of content through discussion and sharing of resources. Properly cultivated and facilitated, the value of the community grows greatly as it ages.

THE FLIPPED MODEL

Laurie Wilson and her husband, Ed, live in the small town of Eden, North Carolina, with their four kids. The oldest child, Buddy, began second grade in 2011, and it quickly became clear to Laurie, a schoolteacher, that he was ready for a more advanced level of math than he was getting in the classroom. It was not long after this that she first heard about Khan Academy, which we discussed in the Introduction. Taking advantage of the wealth of math videos on the site, Laurie was able to work with Buddy at home to explore areas of math for which he was ready, but was not getting exposure to in class.

On the surface, Laurie and Buddy's story may seem to have nothing to do with the world of adult learning, but in fact it points to two key issues in the world of continuing education and professional development. One of these is perennial and primarily educational in nature; namely, that people come to traditional educational classes and events with significant differences in prior knowledge and experience. This is a problem because what people are able to learn is based to a great degree on what they already know—and, of course, these differences in knowledge and experience tend to increase with age. What Buddy is experiencing at this point is only the beginning. In too many cases, lecturers and facilitators have to somehow strike a balance between bringing a certain portion of the adult learners in a class (whether online or off) up to speed while providing enough value to not waste the time of more advanced learners. The comments I have heard from interviewing many lifelong learners over the years suggest that this balance is not particularly easy to achieve.

Another pervasive issue—one that spans both education and business—is that millions of adults are going online each day and finding free content that meets specific learning needs. In the case of Khan Academy, the majority of the content is aimed at the K–12 level, but an increasing amount focuses on adult-level topics. And of course Khan is joined by hundreds, if not thousands, of other sites that offer staggering amounts of free or very low-cost content. Most learning providers have felt the impact of this phenomenon to at least some extent. One of its most common symptoms from a business standpoint is increasing downward price pressure on traditional content-driven educational products.

The Flipped Model recognizes and embraces these two issues. The model's name derives from the "flipped classroom" trend that is taking hold in K–12 and higher education largely because of what Khan Academy and similar efforts have made possible. The basic idea behind the term "flipped classroom" is that what used to occur in the classroom (i.e., lectures) takes place at home, while what used to take place at home (i.e., the student doing homework to apply concepts from lectures) can now be facilitated on a much deeper and more individualized level in the classroom. In Buddy Wilson's case, this would mean that he could pursue more advanced levels of math while still receiving meaningful support in a classroom where his peers may not be at the same level.

The Flipped Model also draws inspiration from the new wave of "content marketing" that is rapidly gaining ground across the business world. The idea behind content marketing is that businesses provide a steady stream of articles, blog posts, videos, and other helpful content—most of it educational in nature—to prospects *before* they ever make a purchase. By doing this, the business raises awareness, builds trust and authority, and establishes the value of its offerings. Educational businesses can enjoy these same benefits while using content as a path to paid offerings that offer a deeper, more interactive, and more intimate experience based on the content. These experiences may take the form of traditional seminars or conference sessions, but they may also take more individualized forms such as mentoring, coaching, or customized training experiences. They may also involve the learner earning continuing education credit, which is not available from the free versions of the content. In all cases, learners have access to substantial content *prior* to the formal learning experience that is the core of the revenue model.

Where It Works

In theory, the Flipped Model can work in any situation in which traditional seminar, conference session, mentoring, or coaching models might apply, but it is particularly powerful for what I characterize as "jumpstart" and "mastery" situations. In jumpstart situations, relative novices—for example, people who are early in their careers or who are making a career switch—need to get up to speed quickly. In mastery situations, more advanced learners want to reach levels of knowledge and skills that they may find difficult achieving on their own. In either case, lectures, reading, and other forms of structured content are an educationally effective way to convey core concepts and build excitement, while more interactive and intimate modes of learning can help learners with critical thinking and applications.

In addition to serving specific types of learners well, the Flipped Model can also be a powerful addition to an organization's portfolio in markets where competition for offering various forms of continuing education (CE) credit is high and content has become commoditized. By their nature, the experiences delivered as part of the Flipped Model are difficult for competitors to replicate. The value they deliver is higher and much more differentiated than typical CE offerings. In most cases, the price can and should be commensurately higher to reflect this value and the additional effort it will typically require from an expert facilitator.

Downsides and Upsides

The main downside to the Flipped Model is that it involves the creation and distribution of a significant amount of content *prior* to customers paying for a learning experience. While technology has made this sort of production and distribution dramatically easier, it still requires direct financial investment and/or time along with the risk that the investment may not pay off. While there are ways to offset this risk, they should be pursued with caution. The first is to "borrow" content from other sources. There is no reason, for example, that videos from TED-Ed (http://ed.ted.com/) or Khan Academy (www.khanacademy.org) or other sources could not be used as the basis for a Flipped Model experience. But it is difficult to build the same level of value for your own brand with borrowed content that you would with content you create, and a strong brand is particularly important in situations where you may want to charge a premium price. Additionally, you could charge for at least some of the content that paves the way to the main learning experience in the Flipped Model. This may be an effective approach both for generating some additional income and for filtering out learners who may not value a higher-end experience, but it also will almost certainly cut down on broad sharing of your content and the opportunities and prospects that may come from that sharing.

A major upside of the Flipped approach is that it combines a very natural process for building brand visibility, trust, and authority with the potential for delivering distinctive learning experiences that reinforce your value even as they are difficult for competitors to replicate. These are not the kinds of offerings for which customers go searching for cheaper options. They are the kinds of offerings that lead to long-term loyalty, repeat business, and ongoing referrals from your customers. Moreover, putting free content into the market is a way of demonstrating your value *and* determining whether you are hitting the mark and precisely how you can deliver additional value. The Flipped approach fits very well into the whole cycle of listening, asking, and testing described in the previous chapter.

THE VIRTUAL CONFERENCE MODEL

As I am writing this book, *Social Media Examiner*, an online magazine focused on helping marketers leverage social media, is about to launch its fourth Social Media Success Summit virtual conference. Three thousand people attended the 2011 conference, and based on information in e-mails from *Social Media Examiner* founder Michael Stelzner, the event is on track to match or exceed that number—at $595 per ticket. The Social Media Success Summit takes place over the course of a month and features a roster of speakers that is basically a "who's who" in the world of social media marketing. It also leverages the LinkedIn social media networking platform to support a vibrant community around the conference. All of this occurs, of course, without either the attendees or the speakers having to leave the comfort of their homes or offices.

I should mention, too, that *Social Media Examiner* itself is only four years old. This is an example of the "Any Given Monday" phenomenon that I referenced back in Chapter 1. Based on a combination of acumen, experience, and access to free or low-cost technologies, founder Michael Stelzner was able to build an audience that rivals that of the highly popular Mashable website and launch an event that is on par with anything the American Marketing Association or other large, traditional organizations might provide. From a revenue model standpoint, the Social Media Success Summit actually adheres to traditional conference models in simply charging a fee for attendance as its primary revenue source, but the overall business model represents a dramatic disruption of traditional event business models as a result of the high degree of accessibility and convenience it provides for attendees and the much lower resource structure it enables for *Social Media Examiner*. Similar to the Flipped Model, the Virtual Conference Model is an instance in which a shift in what technology makes possible has been significant enough to transform a traditional model into something quite different.

I asked Social Media Examiner *founder Michael Stelzner about the factors that have driven the success of the Social Media Success Summit. One clear reason is the larger trend in business to cut back on travel expenses. Here's what Stelzner said:*

It's become extremely successful because as I have been doing this, businesses have been reducing their outrageously high cost of going to events (taking time off from work, traveling, etc.). By eliminating all of that with a virtual conference, we were able to reduce the price point quite a bit as well. It was a win-win because we could have a much lower price point of, say, $300 instead of, say, $600, and we could sell significantly more tickets at a much higher profit margin because we could sell them globally, not being geographically constrained. And that's become the core of *Social Media Examiner*. We've got all these big events three times a year and we usually get at least 1,000 to 3,000 people coming to these events live. Instead of them taking place all day long, they take place over an entire month, and that's been very well received by our audience.

Get the full interview with Michael Stelzner at www.learning-revolution.net/podcast/.

Virtual conferences typically rely on a range of technologies, whether integrated into a single, cohesive platform or linked together more loosely. At a minimum, most rely upon webinar or webcast technologies to deliver a lineup of sessions similar to what you would find at a typical conference. Many conferences also incorporate text-based chat technologies, social media tools, and discussion forums as ways for attendees to interact with each other and with session leaders. Some of the more sophisticated virtual conferencing platforms offer 3-D-type environments and tradeshow capabilities, enabling vendors to post marketing materials and graphics, communicate with visitors to their designated area within the platform, and gather leads. My research at my firm, Tagoras, suggests that the results from this last set of tools have been mixed so far, but I have little doubt that as the tools improve and vendors and customers become more knowledgeable about how to use them effectively, they will become an important part of the virtual conference mix.

Where It Works

A virtual conference can be used for just about anything a traditional place-based conference can be used for, including an annual meeting of members, customers, or business partners, the launch of new products and services, and of course, delivery of education. In the trade and association world, where annual member meetings are a mainstay, the research we have done at Tagoras shows that adoption of virtual events in general—conferences, trade shows, and business meetings being the main examples—has doubled to tripled over the past year. A number of organizations, ranging from the Healthcare Financial Management Association to the American Nurses Credentialing Center and the Society for Technical Communication, have successfully offered virtual events focused on the delivery of education. (For more on this trend, visit www.tagoras.com/virtual-events.) Even so, it appears that the vast majority of associations have still not tried virtual conferences at this point. Considering that most of the typical association's members do not make it to the organization's flagship annual meeting, this seems like an area ripe for growth—or one where the role of annual meetings will be displaced by competitors or other formats.

Downsides and Upsides

Not surprisingly, the potential downside most often mentioned when I discuss virtual conferences with my clients is the loss of interaction and intimacy that they feel comes with the medium. It's tempting to simply dismiss this perception as outdated. People, after all, have become dramatically more accustomed to interacting in meaningful ways online since the rise of Facebook and other popular social media. Certainly, the evolution of social media in general has made the virtual conference much more attractive. Even so, there is often a very real loss that occurs when human beings don't have the opportunity to communicate in person. To a certain extent, this can be offset by use of video technologies along with social tools, but I don't think this problem will ever be eliminated. As a result, it seems unlikely that virtual conferences or other virtual events will entirely replace face-to-face learning, particularly for organizations with a long-established tradition of face-to-face meetings. Still, to not provide a virtual option means not providing a significant new learning opportunity to the large percentage of the organization's audience that may never come to an annual meeting.

Another perceived downside—one specific to organizations that already offer traditional meetings—is that virtual conferences may "cannibalize" attendance at the existing face-to-face meetings. Having now worked with or interviewed a wide range of organizations that offer both face-to-face and virtual conferences, I have yet to find any evidence for the cannibalization argument. Indeed, the situation in many cases seems to be exactly the opposite—the presence of a virtual conference actually increases attendance at face-to-face conferences. One key reason for this may be that the virtual event raises awareness of the organization in general and the value it can offer. In any case, if an organization does experience a significant decline in attendance at face-to-face meetings following the introduction of a virtual conference, I'd argue that this is a sign that a virtual event is better aligned to the value the organization's audience is seeking. To stay relevant and continue growing, it is a good idea to follow that sign.

A big slice of the value for attendees at a virtual conference is, of course, that it does not require either the expense or the time associated with travel. It is simply hard to beat the convenience of staying in your office or at home while still getting access to great content and interaction with peers. For many people, this will mean taking advantage of learning opportunities that they simply would not have even considered before.

For providers, a huge upside is not having to deal with the logistics and planning that are required for place-based events. This is not to say that a great deal of planning and organization are unnecessary for holding a successful virtual conference, but taking geography out of the equation makes a big difference. Very often—depending on the exact nature of the event—this can result in a dramatically lower cost model. Many providers choose to pass along at least some of these cost savings to attendees in the form of lower registration fees, but even with lower fees, margins are often significantly higher.

THE MASSIVE MODEL

If there is one thing the Internet offers that makes it stand apart from any previous form of communication, it is the ability to communicate on a global scale at practically no cost. In the world of education, this capability has led very naturally to distributing content on a much broader basis than was previously possible, and also to promoting a level of interaction and collaboration among experts and learners previously unheard of. Now, what if these capabilities were channeled into a single, large-scale learning experience? That's what the Massive Model is all about.

Massive learning experiences combine a structure and content assembled by one or more experts with a very high degree of participation and interaction by large numbers of learners. The experience may take place within a single day, but more typically extends over a longer period of time, and the "content" that is created by learners as the experience unfolds is often as important as anything contributed by the experts who facilitate the experience.

I first tuned in to the Massive Model when I noticed that Stephen Downes and George Siemens, two Canadian thought leaders in the world of learning and technology, were launching a large-scale online course experience to facilitate learning about a concept they call "connectivism"; in a nutshell, the idea that knowledge resides as much in our connections to others as it does in our own heads. The course was open to anyone, and though it was based on a twelve-week curriculum structured by Downes and Siemens, it was clear from the beginning that the whole point was to demonstrate connectivism in action—that is, much of the value of the course would be generated by the connections it helped form and the content and conversations those connections sparked. As hundreds, and ultimately thousands, of people around the world rushed to sign up, the experience was dubbed a "massive open online course," or MOOC. All content in the course was made available through RSS feeds, and students could choose to participate in a variety of ways: through discussion board, blog posts, videos, web conferences, and even the 3-D virtual environment Second Life. Students could "tag" the ideas, reflections, and other digital content they created and it would automatically be pulled into a combined RSS feed and e-mail newsletter for the course. (You can still search on the tag "CCK11," for example, and find pages of student contributions to the course.)

I asked George Siemens, who along with Stephen Downes launched the first experience labeled a MOOC, about what made the timing right for the concept to catch on. Here's his response:

What was the particular reason for why it captured a bit of interest? I think it's a lot of things. Sometimes you get this sense that there is really something novel happening, but then you pull back a little bit and you realize that these things have been going on for a decade or more. What's really novel isn't necessarily any one element; it's just how these things were pulled together. So at that stage, bandwidth was much better than it had been in early 2000 and the software for holding live sessions and lectures was better developed. There was also an increased degree of skill in many education settings. Faculty was more comfortable blogging and participating in open settings. It's all of these things that sort of came together with the skill of faculty being at a higher level, with the technologies being a little more developed. And there was a general increased consciousness in educational settings, at least around different pedagogical approaches and the potential role that technology and the online environment might have.

Get the full interview with George Siemens at www.learning -revolution.net/podcast/.

Siemens and Downes have since gone on to lead other MOOCs, and a number of participants in the original experience have launched their own massive learning experiences. As the MOOC concept was taking hold, I also became aware of how another "massive" model was being used to facilitate a different kind of learning experience. At the Institute for the Future (IFT), game designer Jane McGonigal was making use of a relatively simple set of online tools to tackle very large and complex problems. Earlier, in 2007, McGonigal had been one of the designers for an online "alternate reality" game called *World Without Oil*. Described as a "massively collaborative imagining of the first thirty-two weeks of a global oil crisis,"[1] *World Without Oil* invited players to contribute blog posts, videos, voice mails, and images that worked collectively to create a vision of what the "alternate reality" of a world without oil would really be like. More than 1,500 people did just that over the course of thirty-three days in response to a series of news alerts and scenarios developed and posted by the game designers. The driving idea was that as large groups of people imagine and collaborate their way through an issue like this, and share their reactions and ideas, awareness increases and innovative solutions may emerge.

McGonigal's next major effort of this sort, *Superstruct*, was what caught my eye in 2008. Similar to *World Without Oil*, *Superstruct* asked players to imagine an alternate reality, but this time well out into the future. Participants were asked to create a profile of themselves in the year 2019 and then respond to a series of five "superthreats" over a period of several weeks. These threats included things like major disruptions to the world's food supply and the outbreak of highly infectious respiratory disease. To help tackle these threats, participants were asked to develop "superstructures"—basically, tools, processes, organizations, or other approaches that would ameliorate or possibly even solve the problem. More than 8,000 people participated in this exercise. A catalog of the superstructures they developed remains available at http://archive .superstructgame.net/superstructures.

There was no charge for participation in these massive games or in the course that was offered by Siemens and Downes.[2] In either case, it is possible to imagine revenue being generated through sponsorship or advertising, or possibly through sale of related materials or tools, like a course packet or an app. Directly charging participants may also be an option, particularly in the case of a MOOC, which is more clearly directed at supporting outcomes for the individual learner. What may be a much more compelling revenue path for these kinds of events, however, is one tied to the types of data and analytics they tend to generate. In the case of an experience like *Superstruct*, for example, mining the proposed super-structures and the interactions that led to them may produce valuable insights for companies actively seeking to address the very problems on which the game is based. Or monitoring the performance of students and players may provide a valuable basis for talent scouting—exactly the approach that three robotocists-turned-educational-entrepreneurs are taking with Udacity, a company that is offering free computer science and artificial intelligence classes on a very large scale. The first class attracted more than 160,000 students from 190 different countries. The company has now moved to identifying high-talent individuals in its talent pool and connecting them—for a finder's fee—to high-tech companies that are hungry for more engineers and programmers. Whether this will prove to be a viable business model for the company remains to be seen, but the opportunity it points to is very real. Many types of value can be mined from large-scale learning experiences, and it seems certain we will see the emergence of various ways of monetizing this value in the coming years.

Where It Works

The Massive Model can work wherever there are topics or issues that attract broad interest. Experiences developed around "101" subject areas, emerging trends, or pervasive social issues may all be candidates. In some cases, the Massive Model may also combine well with or replace a traditional conference model.

Downsides and Upsides

The most obvious downside to the Massive Model is that you have to somehow have access to a large enough audience to pull it off. Siemens and Downes had been building a following for years before they launched the MOOC, and they had a natural global network of people who would be fascinated with participating in such an event. McGonigal and IFT also had a following, and they had the power of influential foundations and press coverage on their side. The founders of Udacity are connected to Stanford University and to Google, and thus had significant brand associations to draw upon. Smaller organizations and individual subject matter experts may consider following this lead and forming relationships with brands that already have a large audience. Finally, organizations that already have a larger base of members or customers may have a built-in audience for the Massive Model. Even without a readily available audience, however, news about access to high-quality free content has a way of spreading quickly across the web. Complete unknowns should not, therefore, rule out the possibility of pursuing the Massive Model if they have topic or issue that might be a fit for it.

Another downside to the Massive Model is that it can be very time-intensive while it is taking place. Even with all of the collaboration that may occur among participants, you can't just wind it up and let it go. You have to stay tuned in, participate, and respond to any issues that arise.

Nevertheless, the upside is that if you pull it off, the Massive Model can obviously generate a big impact very quickly. Whether you reach a thousand or 160,000, massive events tend to create excitement and attract attention. They also result in a pool of participants who are logical candidates for follow-on offerings, whether those are more traditional classes and events or offerings based on the other models discussed here.

NOTES

1. See www.worldwithoutoil.org.
2. Though students who wanted credit for the course needed to be enrolled at the University of Manitoba.

CHAPTER 4

STANDING OUT AND DELIVERING VALUE

EVEN WITH A STRONG UNDERSTANDING of your market and a solid business model, increased competition is a fact of life in the new learning landscape. Some of that competition comes from other learning providers, but a great deal of it comes from the sheer volume of information across multiple types of media competing for people's attention. Learners have more choices than ever—an overwhelming number of choices in many instances—and once they have locked into a provider who can provide an appropriate range of options, getting them to switch can be extremely challenging. To succeed, you have to stand out from the competition, offer learners a variety of options for engaging with you to receive substantial value, and price your offerings in a way that makes sense relative to the value you provide and the options you offer.

POSITIONING AND DIFFERENTIATION

You and your products simply must stand out from the competition in some clearly discernible way, or you will find yourself selling based on a combination of luck, marketing dollars, and most likely, continuing pressure to lower price. Of all the topics covered in this book this is arguably the most important, and for many learning providers it is the hardest to get right. It is usually easier and more comfortable to go through the motions that other providers go through rather than do the hard work of identifying and implementing strategies that distinguish you and your offerings. Ironically, it may also feel safer when, in fact, operating in a market without sufficient differentiation is probably the riskiest thing an organization can do.

So how can you differentiate yourself and your products as a learning provider?

Let's start with the assumption that you have something of value to offer and that you are able to articulate a clear set of benefits for your customers. Simply articulating those benefits is often not enough. In most cases, you already have competitors who are capable of articulating similar benefits for their offerings. Even if you happen to be in the enviable position of being first to market, you can rest assured that, based on your success, others will soon follow with the promise of similar benefits. The problem many learning providers face is that their offerings are not any of these three things:

1. **Unique.** When I scan the catalogs of seminars, conference, webinars, online courses, and other offerings in any given field, there is often not a lot to distinguish one provider from another. The topics, presenters, and formats are not terribly different. Everyone is essentially doing the same thing. In some cases, they are doing *literally* the same thing—the same speakers or webinars, for example, show up again and again.

2. **Memorable.** In the many interviews I do with continuing education and lifelong learning customers, I listen carefully for the specifics they offer about learning experiences. Do they provide examples? Do they have stories? It is rare that they do. Most remember their education and training experiences in very vague and generic terms if they remember them all. I don't have the educational content of the learning experiences in mind when I make this point. It's natural that people forget a great deal of the actual content covered. But they do tend to remember

a dynamic presenter, or a remarkable venue, or other things that stood out. Most of their experiences are just not that memorable.

3. **Remarkable.** When something is remarkable, people literally make remarks about it on their own initiative. They talk about it with peers. They recommend it. If they are channel partners or affiliates, they promote it enthusiastically. This is the highest-impact and most cost-effective form of promotion an organization can have. In my experience, it's not a benefit that many learning providers are enjoying.

How can you make these things happen? A key component, of course, is making sure that you truly *do* have something valuable to offer and that the quality of your offerings is high, but a great deal depends upon how you are *perceived* by your audience—particularly in relation to your competitors. Here are seven approaches to developing a market position that helps you stand out from those competitors and grab the attention of your audience. As with the business models covered in the previous chapter, the list is not exhaustive and the suggestions are not mutually exclusive. Use them as a starting point for creating your own distinctive positioning.

1. Exploit Your Strengths: Let's start with the obvious. Most of us, whether as individuals or organizations, have certain advantages that will be attractive to potential customers and that competitors cannot easily replicate. If, for example, you have long years of experience within a particular field or industry, you have valuable perspectives that others do not have. You are an insider, and you need to highlight this fact in everything you do.

If your products are based on extensive research, or you represent a nonprofit membership organization in the midst of a crowded field of commercial competitors, these too are factors that set you apart, but are often not leveraged in the way they might be. I've repeatedly seen organizations that essentially are *the* trade or professional society within their state or even across their entire field compete with commercial education providers as if they were no different. These organizations are giving up their birthright: a sense of *belonging*, perhaps one of the strongest competitive advantages there is.

We're often too close psychologically to the things we know best, and this mental proximity prevents us from seeing the true value we offer. Chip and Dan Heath, in their bestselling book *Made to Stick: Why Some Ideas Survive and Others Die,* refer to this as the "curse of knowledge." This curse can prevent us from seeing and highlighting things that others will see as valuable because we have become accustomed to them and no longer recognize the value. Don't make this mistake. Try to identify the ways in which you can position yourself as the preferred choice for those in the know. This may require bringing in some outside perspective, whether that means a consultant, colleagues from another organization, or simply a friend or spouse. Get these people to help you see the strengths you may not see yourself.

2. Redefine Your Market: In their bestselling book *Blue Ocean Strategy: How to Create Uncontested Market Space and Make the Competition Irrelevant,* W. Chan Kim and Renée Mauborgne describe a process for mapping out the factors on which organizations in a market compete. So long as everyone in the market competes on similar factors—as is very often the case—it is difficult for any one organization to outperform the others. As a result, price often becomes the only basis for competition. Organizations that are able to break out of price competition often do so by changing the emphasis on key competitive factors in the market, removing some factors entirely, or adding in new factors that no one else has thought of. The changes lead them into untapped parts of their current market or into new markets entirely. Cirque du Soleil, for example, broke the traditional boundaries of the circus industry by getting rid of animals, deemphasizing the role of star performers, and adding a story line to their shows. The result, a form of circus aimed much more at adults than at kids, produced extraordinary new revenue opportunities in an industry that was widely perceived as dying.

The University of Phoenix made analogous strategic moves in the market for higher education. Among other changes, it got rid of the traditional, sprawling campus and tenured professors, opting instead for more modest, commuter-friendly locations, online delivery, and a faculty made up largely of working practitioners in each field of study. The result was a higher-education experience that better fit the needs of working adults.

As you think about your potential offerings, ask yourself where you can change the emphasis, take away typical competitive elements, or add new elements entirely. One of the reasons virtual conferences have gotten traction in many markets is that they eliminate one of the traditional areas of emphasis for meetings and events: the destination. This is more than just a matter of embracing cutting-edge technology. It fundamentally changes both the value component and the resource component of the overall business model. Customers no longer have to spend time and money to travel, which is a significant value enhancement. In addition, because social technologies have improved dramatically and most people feel much more comfortable with them, the value of interaction received in comparison to that of traditional conferences drops only somewhat, if at all, for many learners. In other words, it is a net win. And, of course, the provider gets the benefit of greatly reduced costs by eliminating most of the logistical hassles associated with a traditional event.

3. Set the Standard: Education and training is an area that naturally lends itself to setting and adhering to standards. To the extent that you or your organization can set the standard for education within your field, it will be hard for competitors to encroach on your position.

In some cases, a standard may be formal. The Project Management Institute (PMI), for example, has set a formal standard for project management with the various certifications it offers. PMI itself provides training to support earning and maintaining the certification. Other providers can also offer training, but they have to conform to standards set by PMI. At this point, PMI essentially "owns" the project management brand and the education associated with it. It would be very difficult for another organization to knock it out of its dominant position.

In other cases, a standard may be de facto. Think, for example, of what TED has done in establishing a conference format aimed at people interested in creativity, design, and innovation. The standard it has set for short, high-impact presentations has raised the bar for organizations that want to engage a similar audience. Or consider what The Teaching Company, a business that generates more than $100 million in revenue annually, has done in the market for high-quality arts and sciences and enrichment content. The company has developed an intensive selection process in which only 1 in 5,000 of the college and university faculty vetted for creating a course are actually selected. The result is a very high level of quality and customer satisfaction that has kept The Teaching Company a leader in its niche even as free options have proliferated across the web.

4. Be Contrarian: In the world of software, companies often find themselves caught in a continual grind to meet customer demands for new features and products. A company called 37signals took the opposite approach, purposely limiting the range of features it offers on a range of products that itself is relatively limited. By taking this simple, focused approach—one that is almost the polar opposite of what most software companies do—37signals has grown dramatically year over year, built a raving fan base of customers, and attracted investment by Amazon founder Jeff Bezos.

This type of thinking also applies to training and education business models. Currently, for example, there is a great deal of focus across most markets on moving education online and creating cheaper, faster, and more convenient on-demand learning experiences. This book is, in many ways, a reflection of that trend, and yet even as I emphasize the use of technology to deliver and enhance learning, I have no doubt there are significant opportunities for creating premium "slow learning" experiences, particularly for more advanced learners, or intensive face-to-face bootcamps for novice learners. Similarly, whether online or off, many trade and professional associations operate under the assumption, whether explicit or implicit, that they must be all things to all members. This often results in a large catalog of mediocre offerings, when in fact both members and the organization might be better served by focusing on and excelling in a much more limited range of topics.

5. Create a Story: From a purely logical standpoint, it makes very little sense to pay three to five dollars for a cup of hot coffee and milk, but millions of people gladly do just that on a daily basis at Starbucks. The key is that they aren't just buying coffee: they are buying into a story, one in which they are a bit special, the type of person who enjoys a European-style coffee experience in comfortable, nicely designed surroundings—even if they will be simply rushing out the door to work with their double decaf skinny Venti mocha. As Starbucks has grown, it has struggled to maintain this sense of story, but even now, the story is a large part of what keeps people coming to Starbucks as opposed to significantly less costly options now offered through McDonald's and other chains.

In the world of higher education, the prices Ivy League institutions are able to charge are only partly connected to the quality of the education they provide. When you buy into Harvard or Yale, you are buying into a story, one that connects you with wealth, influence, and some of the great names in American history.

Customers may or may not be conscious of the stories that drive the value of particular products or brands, but stories are powerful nonetheless because they connect so directly to our self-image. Indeed, there is substantial evidence that even minor changes to the stories we live and work by can have a substantial impact on our behavior. Drawing on a range of such evidence in his book *Redirect: The Surprising New Science of Psychological Change*, University of Virginia psychology professor Tim Wilson demonstrates how different narratives shape our lives and how "story prompts" often serve to direct people down particular paths.[1] As Wilson makes clear, "prompts" do not necessarily have to be complex. Indeed, simple often works best. One potential approach in the world of education is to provide learners with a "roadmap" that helps them see how your offerings take them from point A to point B.

This is exactly what CAI—a human resources, compliance, and people development organization based in Raleigh, North Carolina—accomplishes with a tool called The Management Advantage (see Figure 4-1). The tool helps learners identify the knowledge and competencies they need based on their current role in their organization as well as the new knowledge and competencies they need to acquire as their careers progress. The Management Advantage thus serves the double purpose of providing learners with a coherent "narrative" for their learning and providing an important role for CAI in that narrative.

Figure 4-1

The Management Advantage™
Learn, Grow, Succeed

Individual Contributors | Team Leaders | Supervisors | Managers | Directors and Experienced Managers

Stepping Up to Supervision Certification Program	Team Leader Certification Program	Newly Appointed Supervisor Certification Program	Fundamentals of Management Certification Program	Practical Management I Certification Series	Practical Management II Certification Series	Leadership Essentials Certification Program
Topics Covered: Moving from Individual Contributor to Supervisor Assessment and Development for Future Role Managing Tasks and People Planning and Goal Setting Time Management Motivating and Setting Clear Expectations Demonstrating Leadership as an Individual Contributor	Topics Covered: Role of the Team Leader Characteristics of an Effective Leader Communicating Your Message Resolving Conflict and Handling Difficult People Providing Performance Feedback Motivating and Improving Employee Productivity Training for Results	Topics Covered: Role of the Supervisor Making the Transition Planning Your Team's Goals Delegating the Work Principles of Effective Communication Communication Styles Handling Conflict Motivation and Recognition	Topics Covered: Effective Leadership Actions and Behaviors Creating a Leadership Vision Multilevel Influence Situational Leadership Effective Two-Way Communication Developing Feedback Messages Coaching Fundamentals Establishing and Maintaining Credibility	Courses Included: Improving Communication Using the DISC Assessment Maximizing Performance: The Power of Feedback Developing Others Through Coaching Inspiring Employee Motivation Workplace Laws for Managers and Supervisors Interviewing for Success Managing Problem Performance Conducting Effective Performance Appraisals	Courses Included: Building Relationships Using the Myers-Briggs Type Inventory Creative Problem-Solving Managing Conflict in the Workplace Building Successful Teams Time Management: Analyze, Strategize, and Attack Steps to Delegating Effectively Leading Productive Meetings Managing Change	Topics Covered: Translating Strategy into Action Building Strategic Relationships Leveraging Your Emotional Intelligence Leading Through Change Developing Employee Capability
Two consecutive full days	Two consecutive full days	Two consecutive full days	Two consecutive full days	Four full days (eight three-hour courses held over two months) Three-hour courses may be taken individually	Four full days (eight three-hour courses held over two months) Three-hour courses may be taken individually	Five full-day sessions held over three months

Copyright © CAI. Reprinted with permission.

As Colleen Cunningham, CAI's director of learning services, explains,

> The feedback from our customers has been one of relief since CAI created The Management Advantage curriculum model. Rather than having them look at a list of courses on our website, we have made their lives much simpler by packaging the training content. As a result, they can easily see how the model lines up with their company's organizational structure. They can then quickly assess which of their employees need which level of training within the model. In addition, the model showcases an uncomplicated career progression path for developing their employees.

What story can you tell, and how can you frame it in a way that provides a clear and easy path to value for your customers?

6. Imitate Strategically: While innovation is all the rage in business circles these days, it does not always pay to be the innovator in your field. In fact, it doesn't even pay *most* of the time. In his 2010 book *Copycats: How Smart Companies Use Imitation to Gain a Strategic Edge*, Ohio State University professor Oded Shenkar cites a study that examined business model innovations and other breakthroughs occurring over a period of more than fifty years and found that 97.8 percent of innovation value goes to the imitators, not the original innovators.[2] One of the ways to leverage the innovation of others is to borrow their innovations to position yourself within your niche. What if, for example, you implemented something similar to The Teaching Company's "1 in 5,000" approach (discussed earlier in this chapter) to developing a standard-setting line of content in your market? Similarly, industry- or topic-specific versions of the TED model (first discussed in Chapter 1) can easily be applied in niche markets. (Indeed, this is already happening to a certain extent with initiatives like TEDMED, focused on health and medicine.) Trade and professional associations with state or local chapters could even embrace the TEDx component of the TED model, which provides for localized versions of TED-type events.

In general, positioning does not have to be totally unique; it just has to be distinctive within your particular niche, which provides wide latitude in capitalizing on the success of others.

7. Adapt Creatively: Back in the days when I first stumbled into the world of learning and technology I was working on a doctorate in comparative literature at the University of North Carolina. One thing you realize quickly as a comparatist is how much writers borrow not only from each other, but also from other art forms. In my own research, for example, I studied a number of poets who took many of the principles of cubist painting and applied them in their poetry. In many cases, this resulted in poems that are now—for good reason—largely forgotten. In the hands of brilliant poets like William Carlos Williams, however, the creative adaptation of principles of visual art resulted in truly remarkable work.

Creatively adapting ideas, principles, or tools from areas seemingly unrelated to your business can also be a powerful way to develop a unique positioning. One story in this vein that I have enjoyed seeing unfold over recent years is that of Gary Vaynerchuk. The son of Russian immigrant parents, Vaynerchuk grew up working in the family liquor business in New Jersey. Along the way, he became fascinated with wine and set out to learn everything he could about it. Given that he was only 16 and not of legal drinking age when he first discovered his passion, Vaynerchuk trained his palate "backward" by tasting as many of the flavors ascribed to wine as he possibly could. Over time, he built up tremendous knowledge. Later, when Gary was looking for ways to grow the family business, he noticed the growing popularity of Internet video and realized he could leverage video to share his wine knowledge. The result? Wine Library TV, an ongoing series of broadcasts similar to the brief segments you might see in a human interest or culture segment on the nightly news. The response was tremendous, and Gary has gone on to attract legions of followers. His thousandth episode, posted in the spring of 2011, attracted nearly four thousand comments, and Wine Library TV has spawned a highly active online community of "Vayniaks" on its forums (http://forums.winelibrary.com). Needless to say, Vaynerchuk is now very uniquely positioned in the wine business—and all because he was paying attention to developments *outside* of the wine business. With this unique positioning, he has grown revenues in the family business from $4 million annually to more than $60 million annually.

How Not to Differentiate

If you put some time into it, you will no doubt be able to come up with other ways in which you could differentiate your offerings. There are, however, areas that should be avoided whenever possible.

Price is the most important of these, or more specifically, *low* price. Indeed, most of the point of differentiation and effective positioning is to avoid having to compete on price. Once you go down the road of lowering prices or frequently discounting to stay ahead of competitors, it is hard to turn back. It is important to recognize, too, that assuming costs stay constant, a reduction in price typically results in an even greater reduction in net revenue. By cutting prices in the short term, you cut into the long-term viability of your business. This is not to say that you should ignore price as a positioning factor. The less differentiated your offerings are along other lines, the more you will have to make sure that you are not too far out of alignment with competitor pricing. Nonetheless, unless you are out to completely corner a market with penetration pricing that knocks competitors out of the game, low pricing should not be a major part of your positioning. (And if you are going for market share, be sure you can sustain low prices for as long as necessary and then have a plan for raising them over time.)

I am also skeptical of convenience as a *primary* source of differentiation. As I noted earlier, convenience has to be taken into account when developing business models, but this is different from competing over the long term on the basis of convenience. Like lowering price, convenience tends to be too easy for potential competitors to replicate. If you are a local provider with no other direct competitors in your area, it may make sense to emphasize convenience initially, but even then be aware that you have no control over whether a competitor decides to move in and capitalize on convenience. Over the longer run, you need to differentiate in a way that is more difficult for your potential competitors to copy.

THE VALUE CONTINUUM

Let's assume that you have managed to develop a uniquely positioned offering, one that will deliver tremendous value to the learner. Having done this, you will be well ahead of most of the competition, but there still is a challenge: A huge part of your market at this point probably isn't ready to buy from you *or* your competition. They may not know you; they may not trust you; they may not understand the value you have to offer. In addition, even the prospects you do manage to convert into customers may only engage with you periodically, perhaps participating in a course or discussion one day, but then focusing their attention elsewhere for days, weeks, or even months after that. So, what now? Time to embrace the number one maxim of selling in the new learning landscape:

Demonstrate value early, easy, and often.

Early: The sooner you can provide a prospect with evidence that you are the real thing and have something of exceptional value to offer, the better. Think of how relationships start in your own life. It's often a series of small but thoughtful gestures that lead to conversation and ultimately to friendship. Someone holds the door for you, or lends you a pen when you need one; a brief conversation here, a deeper discussion there, over time leading to friendship. Too often we try for a sale the first time someone lands on our website or reads our brochure, but doing this can mean that we never get a second opportunity.

Easy: Don't make it difficult for prospects to get access to some of the value you offer. Don't make them pay, and don't make them hand over personal information, particularly in the early stages. ("I will hold the door for you if you will provide me with your name and e-mail address." "Uh, no thanks. I can manage.") We have a tendency to think of marketing and selling as akin to hunting. Indeed, salespeople within organizations are often classified as hunters or farmers. The hunters are the ones that go out after new business, while the farmers cultivate existing customers. But customers rarely are comfortable feeling like a target—it makes for a tense, uneasy relationship that may never grow. In today's world, it makes more sense to adopt the farming model right from the beginning.

Often: Years ago when I was studying and then teaching Russian, one of the mantras in the classroom was "Repetition is the mother of learning." That's wisdom that applies well not just in the classroom, but also in the market for knowledge and education. Prospects need to learn about you and your products, and one of the best ways for them to do this is through multiple experiences with the value you provide. Similarly, even for existing customers, you need to strive to fill the gaps that may occur between formal learning experiences. Don't stop providing additional value simply because you have made the first sale. Stay in touch in meaningful ways, whether through blogging, e-mail newsletters, social networks, videos, or other media.

One word of caution: Don't confuse frequency with value. Just because you can contact prospects and customers doesn't mean you should. As a general rule, the method and frequency of contact should be determined by your audience and not by you. This is a key reason why it is important to use a variety of different communication channels; customers can opt in to whatever works best for them. Your job is to make sure you provide value wherever they happen to tune in.

The Accelerant Curve

One of the most elegant tools I have encountered for envisioning and plotting out your value continuum is the Million Dollar Consulting® Accelerant Curve, developed by bestselling author and "Million Dollar Consultant" Alan Weiss. A pioneer of value-based pricing, Weiss created the curve to illustrate the relationship between price and other factors like product differentiation and the level of access you provide to knowledge and expertise. While it is aimed primarily at consultants, that shouldn't deter nonconsultants from using it: The principles of the Accelerant Curve apply lock, stock, and barrel to any individual or organization that is in the knowledge and education business.

While I have included an illustration of the curve here, the best way to understand it is to actually plot one of your own. Whether on a piece of paper or a digital device, draw a standard vertical axis and horizontal axis (i.e., a right angle) with a curve starting at the top left and running to the bottom right (see Figure 4-2). The vertical axis represents decreasing barriers to entry. The horizontal axis represents increasing fees and what Weiss characterizes as "intimacy," which basically means greater access to you and the unique value you offer.

The idea, then, is to plot the various ways in which you provide value along this curve. Even when you have (or *think* you have) only a single paid offering, this exercise will help you better see how you can effectively lead prospects toward that offering.

Figure 4-2   Accelerant Curve

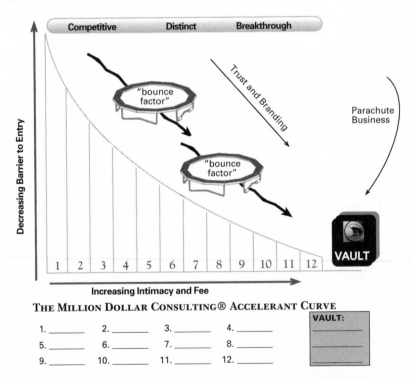

THE **Million Dollar Consulting**® **Accelerant Curve**

Source: Alan's Blog, "Million Dollar Consulting® Accelerant Curve," http://www .contrarianconsulting.com/million-dollar-consulting-accelerant-curve/, © Summit Consulting Group, Inc. Reprinted with permission.

At the top left would be things that are free or low cost. These are easy for anyone to access and serve as a way of demonstrating value to prospective customers. They provide solid value, but their value is relatively generic and the level of access to expertise they offer is relatively superficial. A podcast, a white paper, a free webinar, or, for that matter, this book, would all be representative of potential offerings that fall in the upper to middle-left part of the Accelerant Curve. (Note that "relative" is a keyword when talking about the Accelerant Curve. Everything on your curve should offer meaningful value. It's just that value increases as price rises.)

Moving down the curve, offerings become increasingly differentiated from competing alternatives; access to expertise is much more in-depth; value increases; and price rises. This may mean, for example, moving from informational webinars to an annual event and then to specialized, niche seminars, and customized education and consulting. At the bottom right is what Weiss calls "The Vault"—one or more offerings representing highly differentiated value that only you or your organization can deliver.

VERSIONS AND DERIVATIVES

Fundamental to the concept of the Accelerant Curve is that you provide your customers and prospective customers with *options*. But if you don't already have a number of products developed—and possibly even if you do—you may be wondering how you can possibly fill in the points along an Accelerant Curve. One of the keys is to consider the ways in which you offer different levels of value based upon a single, core product. If, for example, you have developed a classroom-based workshop that you feel is of particularly high value, there are a number of ways that you can either add value to or remove value from similar but distinct products. You might create brief blog posts or articles based on major topics in the workshop and use these to fill in the upper-left part of the curve. In short, there are nearly always opportunities for creating versions of derivatives from products you have developed. Indeed, you should build this potential into your planning for the products. By doing this you provide a variety of ways for your prospects and customers to engage with you no matter where they are in need for training and readiness to make a purchase.

PRICING

There is a reason I covered concepts like positioning and the value continuum before coming to the issue of pricing: Pricing for knowledge and learning is highly variable, and will depend—even more so than for other types of goods and services—on the perception of the buyer. By offering a range of ways in which you provide value, and various options for any given offering, you create a degree of pricing flexibility that will be valuable to your customers and will also spare you a great deal of anxiety in establishing the one "right price."

All of that said, you do obviously have to put a clear price tag on each option. So, what is the best way of going about establishing this price? The typical advice is to establish your cost and then work forward by adding an appropriate profit margin and checking yourself against competitors. I call this the "downside pricing" approach: It's great for making sure you don't lose your shirt, but it is also likely to result in your leaving a lot of money on the table. Pricing is ultimately about what the market will bear; in other words, the amount of value customers place on your expertise. If you price a product at fifty dollars and customers are quite willing to pay seventy-five, you are losing money even if you are covering costs and achieving your target margin.

The alterative is "upside pricing," which is based on the value of the offering rather than on intrinsically limiting approaches like underlying costs or time and materials. The keys to successfully implementing upside pricing include:

◆ Making the time and effort to understand customers' needs and the value they place on these needs. As noted, these conversations are different from the "What courses do you want" questions that are typical on needs assessment surveys. Indeed, this is one area in which one-on-one conversations are often of much more use than surveys. If you help the customer achieve specific learning objectives, what value will be created? Will there be career advancement possibilities? Will the customer be able to earn more revenue from her customers as a result of greater expertise or the ability to offer new products or services? Probing along these lines will help both you and the customer determine more clearly what the real value of the educational experience is. In some cases—for example, a pay raise—the value is highly quantifiable. In other cases, it will be much less so, but even in fuzzy areas like "career advancement," customers often have an intuitive answer when asked "What's that worth to you?" Even if the answer is not put in terms of dollars, it will usually provide some indication of the level and type of motivation of customers. The higher the level of motivation, and the more it is intrinsic rather than extrinsic, the greater the value the customer is likely to place on an offering.

◆   Testing can also be an important tool in determining price. You can test directly by actually attempting to presell an offering at a particular price or prices. Or, less directly, the level of demand you experience during the testing phase is a useful indicator of what you may ultimately be able to charge for a product. Obviously, the stronger the demand, the more flexibility you may have in setting a price.

◆   Clearly differentiating your product from the competition is another key factor. Embracing upside pricing does not mean that you completely ignore the competition, but it does mean that your analysis of the competition becomes as much or more about value than about price. How can you position yourself in a way that clearly suggests value well above and beyond that of the competition? The more effectively you differentiate, the less tied you are to any pricing anchors that the competition has set in the market.

◆   Offering differing levels of value and pricing along your Accelerant Curve gives you some protection against both underpricing and overpricing. Customers who are price sensitive have the opportunity to purchase at a lower price, while customers who want more value and are willing to pay for it have access to higher-cost opportunities. By monitoring purchasing activity along the Accelerant Curve over time, you can recalibrate pricing and value as necessary to get the balance right.

It must be stressed that while upside pricing is dependent upon creating a strong perception of value, you must also be prepared to deliver fully on that value. Upside pricing does not, in the end, give license for simply charging high prices, or worse, gouging your customers. Aside from the obvious ethical implications of doing this, you simply will not be able to create a sustainable, long-term business. The ideal situation is to create a price or range of pricing that is as accessible as possible to your buyers while still representing the high value you offer and providing a healthy margin. While this approach may not offer the mathematical comfort of cost-based or time-and-materials approaches to prices, it nearly always provides for much more substantial net revenue to help fuel your ongoing business growth.

NOTES

1. Timothy D. Wilson, *Redirect: The surprising new science of psychological change* (Hachette Book Group, Kindle Edition, 2011) p. 14.
2. Oded Shenkar, *Copycats: How smart companies use imitation to gain a strategic edge* (Boston: Harvard Business Press, 2010).
3. Tony Clark uses the term "creative adaptation" in a similar way in a series of blog posts published in 2007 on Success from the Nest.

CHAPTER 5

LEARNING BY DESIGN

AS I HAVE ALREADY SUGGESTED throughout the book, the barriers to entering the market for knowledge and education products are lower than they have ever been before. While this means there are tremendous opportunities, it also means that a lot of junk is entering the market. Chances are that you yourself have suffered through long, wandering webinars or pointless podcasts, or have attended seminars that are 95 percent fluff and 5 percent substance. While it is inevitable that quality in the broad market for learning will be highly variable, creating a long-term, profitable education business within your particular niche demands that you understand and apply key principles of learning. Doing so is the only way you can ensure that you actually deliver the high value you promise and on which your reputation and pricing are based.

INTEGRATING LEARNING AND BUSINESS OBJECTIVES

There is a tendency in education markets to think of instructional design—the process by which effective learning experiences are developed—as something that happens separately from overall business strategy. As a result, businesspeople (or even educators, when they wear their business "hats") may advocate products and approaches that do not align with the best possible ways to achieve deliver educational value. (The glut in the webinar market is, in my opinion, a glaring example of this problem.) Conversely, educators may focus purely on how to achieve learning outcomes without any real thought to costs, marketability, operational challenges, or other key business issues. Either approach is a mistake. There needs to be a balance between business strategy and instructional design. Fortunately, there really is no conflict when it comes to striking this balance: The goal from both a business and an instructional standpoint is to ensure that you fulfill your value proposition. In other words, *that the learner actually learns what the learner signed up to learn.*

Viewed from this perspective, instructional design is as much a business tool as it is an educational tool. It helps ensure that a product will, in fact, deliver on its promise, and moreover, do this in the most effective and efficient way. One "magic" ingredient that a good instructional design process brings to product development is clear *learning objectives.*

In simplest terms, a learning objective describes what a student should be able to do after completing a learning activity—in other words, as Robert Mager suggests in his classic, *Preparing Instructional Objectives,* what will the *outcome* be for the student?[1] The following are examples:

- Recite required auditing procedures
- Given appropriate financial documents, identify and document potential revenue recognition problems

These examples share qualities that all good learning objectives should share:

◆ They are *specific* about the *actions* a learner should be able to perform as a result of the learning experience.

◆ They are *measurable*—the actions are ones that an instructor or employer (or, in general, someone besides the student) can see and verify.

Because they are *action-oriented*, good objectives are based on verbs or verb phrases that are open to as little misinterpretation as possible. The following chart from Mager's *Preparing Instructional Objectives* lists phrases that are open to a relatively wide range of interpretations versus those that are not:[2]

Words Open to Many Interpretations	Words Open to Fewer Interpretations
To know	To write
To understand	To recite
To *really* understand	To identify
To appreciate	To sort
To *fully* appreciate	To solve
To grasp the significance of	To construct
To enjoy	To build
To believe	To compare
To have faith in	To contrast
To internalize	To smile

From *Preparing Instructional Objectives: A Critical Tool in the Development of Effective Instruction*, 3rd ed., by Robert F. Mager. Reproduced with permission.

An example of a poor learning objective might be:

To appreciate the significance of the new regulatory initiatives

While an appreciation of new regulatory initiatives may be an overarching goal for a seminar or other learning experience, it is *not specific or measurable enough to serve as an objective.* How will you know that the student has developed an appreciation? Will she be able to recite differences between new regulations and prior regulations? Given a problem based on the regulatory changes, will she be able to solve it? *An effective learning objective requires that the student perform an action that is verifiable by others.*

It is often the case, of course, that learning providers in lifelong learning markets are not in a position to verify that the learner can, in fact, perform the desired action. Nonetheless, your objectives and the instruction you deliver to support them should be such that you are confident a learner would be able to perform the desired action if he or she were asked to. The learner, after all, is likely to notice at some point whether or not she can do what you promised she would be able to do after she completes the experience you provide. Actual results are, without a doubt, the surest way to garner customer loyalty and spark powerful word-of-mouth promotion for your products. Keep in mind, too, that if your educational products are of the sort that support knowledge and performance in the workplace, employers will care about seeing results, too. Indeed, you want them to care because if they care and you can actually deliver the results, you become a *have-to-have* strategic investment rather than a nice-to-have training cost. Good instructional design helps make that happen.

Finally, it is important to recognize that learning objectives do not apply only in well-defined, structured experiences like courses. Even in community models that are built upon numerous intersecting learning experiences—some formal, some not-there should still be overarching learning goals for the community. Structured content within the community should meet objectives that clearly support these goals. The types of content you provide, the way interactive elements like discussion boards are organized, and the way conversations are facilitated should all reflect an overall sense of the objectives that can be achieved by participating in the community.

SEVEN RULES TO TEACH AND FACILITATE BY

While learning objectives are one key factor in creating high-value learning experiences, there are other significant factors you should keep in mind, some of which are particularly important when educating adults.

These apply most readily to structured content like a seminar, a video, or a webcast, but as with objectives, they can and should also inform less structured learning models:

1. Position it
2. Prune it
3. Chunk it
4. Stimulate multiple senses
5. Remember to repeat to remember
6. Make it active
7. Share the responsibility

Position It

As a general rule, adults need to have a solid understanding of *why* they need to learn something. They want to know how it is relevant to their lives. In the best of circumstances, your prospects and customers already have a reasonably clear understanding of their learning needs, are self-motivated to address these needs, and see that whatever you are offering aligns well with achieving their goals. In many instances, however, you will have to make the effort to draw a clearer connection between your offerings and the needs of your audience. In some cases, you may even have to make your audience aware of needs that were not apparent to them. This process begins in your marketing and promotional efforts, but it also extends into the delivery and facilitation of the actual experience. Malcolm Knowles and his collaborators argue in *The Adult Learner* that one of the first responsibilities of facilitators of adult learning is "to help the learners become aware of the need to know."[3] In its simplest form, this involves making clear at the beginning of any structured learning experience what the intended outcomes and benefits are, and to the greatest extent possible, framing these in terms that will resonate with your audience. In addition, wherever possible provide opportunities that help "learners discover for themselves the gaps between where they are now and where they want to be."[4] This may, for example, involve a simple writing exercise in which learners describe in detail the future state they are seeking to achieve and the steps that will be required to get them there. Or it may involve learners engaging in discovery-type learning activities in which they attempt to accomplish a task that requires them to stretch beyond their current knowledge or skill level. However it is accomplished, effectively positioning your offerings—both before and during the actual experience—helps ensure maximum motivation, engagement, and the strongest possible learning outcomes.

Prune It

Each of us as learners has limited "working memory" in our brains for processing new information. There is only so much we are capable of digesting and moving into long-term memory within the context of a specific learning experience. Subject matter experts, on the other hand, usually have a lot to say about the topics they know so much about, and too often they try to convey more information than the audience can really absorb. To teach more, it often pays to say or write less.

Practically speaking, this means taking the time to edit—or have someone else edit—instructional content to get at the core concepts and express these in the simplest possible way. In text, this generally results in:

- Dividing content into segments
- Providing titles and subtitles to indicate each new section
- Shorter paragraphs
- Frequent use of bullet points

It means plenty of white space on the page.

In speaking, it means regular pauses to allow time for ideas to be absorbed.

Visually, it means using images that are unambiguous and relate clearly to the idea being conveyed.

I deliberately use the term "pruning" for this process because when you prune something, you're cutting it back so that it can then thrive even more than it might have otherwise. By removing any ideas, details, images, or other materials that are not *directly relevant* to what you're teaching, you free up some of the information-processing capability available to the learner and provide the learner with more opportunity for associating your ideas with knowledge she already has—an essential step in effective learning.

Chunk It

In addition to pruning materials down to remove anything extraneous, you should try to provide learning in short segments whenever possible. This rule applies especially within the context of longer sessions of structured learning like lectures, webinars, and webcasts. In longer sessions of learning, the average person's mind is likely to start wandering after ten minutes or so focused on one topic or theme.[5] Maintaining attention is critical, because the level of attention a learner devotes to a topic directly impacts learning.

When designing seminars, webinars, or other experiences that rely on a traditional lecture approach, try to divide up the material so that you focus on any particular point for no more than ten to twelve minutes, then shift gears and move to a new point.

Even in situations in which sustaining attention may be less of an issue—for example, when the learner has the freedom to explore a membership learning site at leisure—creating "chunks" of learning is valuable if only because the amount of time the average person can devote to a single session of learning seems to shrink year over year. By providing experiences in which a learner can absorb a significant piece of knowledge within a relatively short space of time, you may help sustain the learner's motivation to learn. We all like to feel that we are making progress and increasing our overall level of competence.

Stimulate Multiple Senses

Take a moment to think about a really great meal you shared with friends or family. What comes to mind? Chances are you visualize the scene in your mind, you hear snippets of the conversation that went on, you can even recall the smells of the food, or perhaps the wine, and taste the last bite of the wonderful dessert that capped off the meal.

All of our senses play a vital role in how we process and remember new experiences and information, but traditional educational experiences, which rely very heavily on learners listening to a lecturer or reading text, often do not take full advantage of this fact. It makes a difference. For example, educational researchers Ruth Colvin Clark and Richard Mayer conducted an analysis of eleven studies that looked at test performance of students who learned from animation and narrative versus narration alone or from text and illustrations versus text alone. In all eleven comparisons, the learners who participated in multimedia lessons—narration with animation, or text and illustrations—did better on a subsequent test than did those who learned from words alone. The multimedia learners did 55 to 121 percent better than those learning from just audio or just text.[6]

Now, there's a catch: You can't just plug random stimulation into your learning experiences and expect it to have the desired impact. Senses have to be engaged in ways that are relevant to the learning experiences. If you're using images in a lecture, for instance, the images and what you say need to be tied together and supportive of each other. Intrusive Microsoft PowerPoint templates or stock photography that is inserted in a page of bullet points simply for decorative purposes not only do not support learning; they may actually detract from it by distracting the learner.

In general, however, providing content in multiple formats is an excellent approach. If you create videos or audio files, provide transcripts or brief summary sheets in writing. Whenever possible, create brief checklists, worksheets, or other items that learners can use to actually apply whatever they may hear or see.

Remember to Repeat to Remember

To firmly establish new information in our long-term memory, we typically need to encounter it many times. This is an innately human need. If you ever watch toddlers or infants as they're trying to learn about something, for example, you'll see that they will repeat the same action over and over, each time taking great interest in the result that is produced (including, often, the reaction from the nearest adult). You may think, *How can they just keep doing that over and over?* But that's part of that learning process for them.

As adults, we don't usually enjoy rote repetition, but nonetheless our brains still require repeated exposure to new concepts and skills as part of the learning process. As a rule, the more complex the learning, the more it requires repetition, and we benefit from this repetition occurring over time and in a variety of contexts. Repetition and contextualization support a process that learning psychologists refer to as "elaborative encoding," which basically means getting new information into our brains in a way that makes it likely to stick. In the context of a single, isolated session of learning—for example, a webinar or a conference session—this need for repetition can be very challenging. Effective teachers must be skilled at presenting new materials from a variety of perspectives, using a variety of examples, over the course of the session. When learning takes place over a longer period of time—through a series of classes, for instance, or in the context of a perpetual learning community—opportunities for repetition are more abundant. Indeed, this is one of the real strengths of the learning community model, but it is a strength we have to consciously leverage. In facilitating a community or teaching a series of classes, we must make a point of repeating the most important points at regular intervals.

As a learning provider, you should build in meaningful repetition opportunities wherever you can. You should also make learners aware of the need for repetition and the reasons why it is important. In particular, it is worth stressing that even information or skills that have seemingly been mastered require review and repetition over time.

Make It Active

Learning is rarely, if ever, a passive activity. We must engage actively with new information as part of the process of moving it into long-term memory. Even simple actions like taking notes during a lecture or while reading can help with this process. So can even brief opportunities to practice what we are learning or to test ourselves in order to determine what we have or have not learned. As already mentioned in this chapter, providing checklists, worksheets, and other tools to accompany instructional content is one simple way to encourage learners to take action. Remember, too, that adult learners tend to be most interested in learning that has immediate relevance to their jobs or personal lives. To the extent that any of the learning activities can draw upon examples and situations that reflect the learner's real-life circumstance, all the better. Similarly, any tools or exercises introduced should be as transferable as possible into the learner's job or everyday life. As Knowles suggests in *The Adult Learner*, your learners are likely to be "life-centered (or task-centered, or problem-centered) rather than subject or content-centered."[7] Keep the learning active and life-centered.

Share the Responsibility

Knowles writes:

> Adults have a self-concept of being responsible for their own decisions, for their own lives. Once they have arrived at that self-concept, they develop a deep psychological need to be seen by others and treated by others as being capable of self-direction. They resent and resist situations in which they feel others are imposing their wills on them.[8]

One of the most significant changes that technology has enabled over the past several years is that we now have so many opportunities for being self-directed learners. In the lifelong learning market as I define it in this book, customers actively embrace that opportunity by making the choice to engage in educational activities (as opposed to participating in mandated training or education, as often is the case in the corporate setting and nearly always is in the K–12 setting). This choice—and the sense of responsibility it implies—should be extended into the learning experience. Making learning active, as covered in the last section, is one way to promote participation and share the responsibility for learning with the learner. Another is to provide as many avenues as possible for the learners to shape learning objectives to increase the relevance of those objectives. A powerful aspect of each of the models for learning I covered in Chapter 3 is that they allow for significant interaction with and among learners, and the feedback gained in this process can shape the course of the experience. Achieving this dynamic in purely self-study situations is much more difficult, but seeking learner input in advance, including through methods already covered in this book, is one important approach, as is providing opportunities for learners to apply knowledge and skills in the contexts that are relevant to them. Even something as simple as a checklist of meaningful "to-do's" to take back to the office can go a long way in supporting this goal.

THE ENDURING POWER OF THE LECTURE

While the lecture as a learning format comes in for a good bit of criticism these days, there are good reasons why it has endured. I asked Monisha Pasupathi, associate professor in developmental psychology at the University of Utah and author of The Teaching Company course How We Learn, to discuss some of those reasons as well as her general perspective on lectures. Here's what she had to say:

Good lectures can take people through an expert's thought process in a way that doesn't happen when you're very interactive. They are really organized, really structured, and really digestible ways to get quite a bit of information in a relatively short time. To acquire the same level of learning from interactive models often will require considerably more time. It often takes considerably more expertise on the part of the teacher or the instructor, because you have to know how to get a group of nonexpert people from Point A to Point B. You have to know where they typically hit a wall in their understanding; what kinds of misconceptions they bring to the table.

The other thought I always have when people talk about being more interactive is that we may have lost the capacity to experience lectures *as interactive*. I remember a really interesting experience I had in Germany where I went to a talk, and it was given in German. And my German wasn't terrific at the time, so I had a hard time processing this lecture, but what I noticed about it was that it was a very old-fashioned lecture. It was given by a professor who had been there before the wall had come down in the former Eastern Bloc, and he spoke in fully articulated sentences for something like forty minutes in beautiful, erudite German. What I think we don't experience anymore is that kind of lengthy oration.

I suspect there was a time when we used to have better skills for this type of experience and for feeling engaged with lectures. We may be going too far into interactivity in such a way that it is actually undermining people's skill at listening to lectures. Because it is, to some extent, something that we *learn* how to do, and I'd hate to see us unlearn that in favor of new instructional methods that have their own value, but also have their own flaws.

Get the full interview with Monisha Pasupathi at www.learning -revolution.net/podcast/.

EVERYONE, EVERYWHERE, ALWAYS LEARNING

So far, I've focused mostly on using a new set of tools to deliver education in a fairly traditional way. Creating and delivering content, whether that means a classroom lecture or a web-based video or any range of other approaches, suggests a one-way street. It puts you in the position of a broadcaster, a traditional teacher with a much larger lecture hall. Yes, by focusing on valid, effective learning principles you have the learner's interests firmly in mind, but you are really only meeting the learner halfway. Leading learning effectively requires an understanding of how the learner can contribute to the equation and how much power learners actually have these days. Certainly this is true if you embrace a learning community as your business model, but it is equally true with other business models. Your customers and prospective customers encounter you in the context of the much broader environment in which they live and learn. It pays to understand the dynamics of this environment.

The Other 80 Percent

While creating and delivering great content is certainly important, understanding how people are likely to find, access, and use that content is at least as important. Largely as a result of our experiences early in life with school, most of us tend to view learning as a formal, structured experience. It is all about teachers, and classes, and degrees. But if you think about it, even in the context of school, much of our learning happens through our seemingly casual interactions with other students—in the hallways, at lunch, during recess. Indeed, as it turns out, most of the learning we do throughout our lives is *informal.* You probably did not, for example, go to a class to learn to walk, or talk, or dress yourself. You learned these and millions of other things through countless interactions with others and the world around you throughout your life. The same is true of the many more specific skills and knowledge you may possess. While you may have received training or participated in specialized education to prepare you for your job, chances are you learned most of what you know about your work simply by doing it.

By some estimates, as much as 80 percent of our learning happens in an informal manner, and a great deal of it is based on our interactions with other people.[9] Why does it matter? It is very often in the context of this other 80 percent that we make decisions about more formal learning opportunities. If you are not there, not engaged, not providing value, then the chances that a prospect will come to see you or your organization as the source to go to for more formal, paid learning experiences diminishes dramatically. This is all the more true if your competitors *are* there, *are* engaged, and *are* providing value. In the world of the 80 percent, providing learning value is one of the most effective forms of marketing you have available to you.

Given this dynamic, it makes a great deal of sense to develop a deep understanding of that 80 percent and how it might be leveraged in relation to your formal learning products and experiences. As Jay Cross, author of *Informal Learning: Rediscovering the Natural Pathways that Inspire Innovation and Performance*, has put it:

> We humans exist in networks. We are part of social networks. Our heads contain neural networks. Learning consists of making and maintaining better connections to our networks, be they social, operational, commercial, or entertainment. Rich learning will always be more than a matter of the bits flowing back and forth, but the metaphor of learning as networking gives us a way to describe how learning can be embedded in work itself.[10]

The only modification I would make to Cross's words—one I suspect he would have no issue with—is to replace "work itself" with "*life* itself." To leverage more of Cross's language from the same book, to be a life-long learner then is "to optimize the quality of one's networks" *through-out life*.

For anyone operating within the lifelong learning marketplace, meeting prospective learners informally within their daily life networks sets the stage for a much more natural path to learning and for a much deeper, long-term relationship. Rather than appearing suddenly as an interruption—a "pitch" that arrives in the mailbox or the inbox—you develop into an integrated aspect of how they acquire and manage knowledge. Achieving this sort of integration requires significantly more thought and potentially a greater investment of resources than does simply buying advertisements or sending direct mail, but it results in a much higher level of credibility, trust, and value than can be generated through interruption learning. It also is again an area where your business objectives of gaining customers and engaging them for the long term dovetail with learning principles—namely, that we are all avid informal, social learners.

THE SOCIAL–MOBILE SHIFT

While informal learning has always been a part of our lives, it has gotten significantly more attention in recent years because the opportunities for it have exploded as a result of social media. Even now, however, the full impact of social technologies is only beginning to be fully appreciated outside of education circles (and, arguably, even within these circles). Most of the buzz around social media has focused on marketing, or on how it is disrupting traditional media businesses like newspapers. When people do wake up to the role of social media as not only a marketing platform, but also—often simultaneously—a *learning* platform, they tend to wonder how they have missed the connection. As bestselling author Dan Pink puts it in his preface to *The New Social Learning*,

> The deepest, most enduring impact of social media might be on *learning*. There's a certain intuitive, forehead-slapping logic to that insight. Of course! In so many ways, learning is a fundamentally social act. From circle time in kindergarten, to study groups in college, to team projects in the workforce, sociability has always greased the gears of learning.[11]

As Pink came to realize, many of the tools of social media—from Facebook to Twitter to YouTube—have become woven into the fabric of our lives. We don't tend to think of them as learning tools, and yet they provide a continuing stream of information and interactions that impact our knowledge and behavior in ways that are sometimes obvious, but often very subtle. Let's take a moment to consider some of the ways in which major social tools can and are being used.

Blogs

As of February 2011, there were more than 156 million blogs in existence.[12] While most of these do not publish new content on a regular basis, they are nonetheless a significant source of information across the web. For businesses—learning providers included—blogs are an easy and obvious path to publishing a continuing stream of helpful, educational content as part of efforts to attract and retain an audience. Regular publishing in this way helps to establish expertise and authority and can significantly help with efforts to rank higher in search engine results.

Twitter

Twitter, the platform for sending out messages of 140 characters or less, has more than 200 million users at the time I am writing this book. Many of these users leverage Twitter as a platform for sending out links to useful resources and following others who do the same. In addition to providing a way to send messages, Twitter's search engine and Twitter directories like Twellow make it possible to find and focus in on people and topics in the areas of most interest to you. Twitter can be a very valuable tool for identifying your audience, unearthing trends and needs, and providing value through sharing links to resources—including your own blog posts—and retweeting resources shared by others.

Facebook

Quickly approaching a billion users, Facebook has become a perpetual presence in the lives of many of its users. Anything people are likely to share, they increasingly share on Facebook—and this includes any experiences or information you happen to contribute. Just as with Twitter, or any other social network, for that matter, Facebook provides a context in which you can demonstrate value and develop the trust and authority that lead to more formal learning opportunities. It is also a place where you can maintain relationships and fill in the gaps that inevitably occur between the times when learners may pay to access your educational offerings.

LinkedIn

While it's easy to think of LinkedIn as mainly a new way to keep your resume posted and fresh, the site also offers a wide variety of groups organized around professional and personal interests. These groups can be a great place to ask questions or demonstrate your expertise and value by answering others' questions. The site—which has more than 160 million users—also features an "Answers" section that allows users to ask and answer questions. This is another great opportunity for demonstrating expertise as well as asking questions that may help you better understand your market.

Google+

Google+, with more than 170 million users, is the search engine giant's latest foray into the social networking arena, but it would be a mistake to view it as merely an attempt to knock Facebook off of its pedestal. Like Facebook, Google+ allows users to maintain profiles, connect with others, and post content, but Google+ is also tightly tied into Google search and is likely to become more so over time. Google has, for example, already introduced "social search" capabilities that incorporate the activities of people in your circles into your search results. If people in your circles have posted recently on items related to your search, these will typically show up very high in your results. Similarly, by creating and building "circles" and actively sharing valuable information you are likely to show up in the search results for people in your circles. Practically speaking, this means you maintain high visibility in the tool most people are using for their day-to-day search needs. (Microsoft, it should be noted, is doing much the same thing with its Bing search engine.) This is one key reason why leading web marketing authorities like Guy Kawasaki and Chris Brogan are now putting the majority of their social networking efforts into Google+. As Kawasaki puts it, "If I were running a business, I would be thinking, 'Why wait until I have to buy real estate in Manhattan? I should get in now and grab all of the followers I can before Google+ hits the mainstream.' "[13]

Pinterest

When speaking recently to an annual gathering of nursing certification organizations, I asked how many audience members were actively engaged on popular social networks like Twitter, LinkedIn, and Facebook. In each case, well under half of the people in the room raised their hands. When I asked about relative newcomer Pinterest, hands shot up from a majority of the people in the room. Clearly this social network for "pinning up" and sharing objects you find across the web has struck a chord. A great deal of Pinterest's appeal is no doubt rooted in the fact that it is so visually oriented—not a small point when you consider that most learning is driven by vision more than any other sense. As a tool for connecting with their audiences and creating value, the opportunities for learning providers to use Pinterest are limited only by imagination. You might pin up infographics (visual presentations of information and concepts), articles, graphics, or other resources related to a particular topic; syllabi or curricula; collections of videos—you name it. Basically any web page can be "pinned," though pages with photos, graphics, videos, or other visual content tend to have the most appeal. Visitors to your pinboard can then comment on your postings and share them.

YouTube

In many ways, YouTube is to the audiovisual aspect of the web what blogs are to the textual aspect. By leveraging YouTube skillfully, you can create valuable "social objects" that people will be eager to share, just as they would share a valuable blog post. Indeed, because audiovisual content tends to have universal appeal, a well-executed video may get significantly more exposure than a purely text-based blog post would get.

All of these tools together—and many others that are available on the web—provide a platform by which you can be in constant contact and conversation with your audience. They also provide avenues for raising awareness about your offerings (at appropriate and relevant times) and for extending and enhancing those offerings by providing channels in which learners can share. It is becoming increasingly standard, for example, for conferences and other learning events to have a Twitter "hashtag," which is a keyword associated with the event preceded by the "#" symbol. By appending this hashtag to their own tweets, anyone attending or interested in the conference can easily share information, insights, and stories from it.

The growing use of smartphones and tablet computers like the iPad take all of this a step further. There are now nearly 500 million smartphone users globally,[14] and nearly 70 million tablets were sold in 2011.[15] All of the social tools already mentioned, and many more, are available on these devices, as are numerous other types of tools and content that can contribute to learning. The combination of social and mobile means that there is now a pervasive, always-on platform for informal learning experiences that integrate into the day-to-day lives of your prospects and customers.

TERMS OF ENGAGEMENT

Terms like "informality" and "integration" should not be taken to imply a total lack of control. Those who sell learning products have never had the level of control that, for example, a corporate training department might have in mandating compliance training for employees. Sales of learning and knowledge products, like sales of most any other products, are a matter of influence. Influence, in turn, can be sustained over the long haul only by developing social capital. An appreciation of informal learning offers the opportunity to build social capital and leverage influence in more productive and meaningful ways. There are four key aspects to managing influence in the context of informal learning interactions:

1. Attention
2. Interest
3. Motivation
4. Outcomes

Attention

While "interruption," as discussed earlier in the chapter, should be minimized in informal settings, you nonetheless have to actually get someone's attention if you expect to engage them for learning or any other activity. Informal interactions provide an environment for the highest-quality attention: attention that is actually based on *value*. A key skill in informal situations is to be able to concisely and quickly articulate value. As such, good copywriting is a valuable skill these days, as is the ability to use images effectively. To be able to frame an idea in an unusual way, pose provocative questions, or make it crystal clear that you have valuable information to offer is an essential skill in the context of learning and knowledge networks.

Interest

Interest flows from the promise of value that attention reveals. The surest way to spark and maintain interest is to actually have something interesting and valuable to share with your prospective audience, whether through content you have created yourself or through items you have curated from others. This requires a level of understanding of the learner's needs that goes beyond typical "spray and pray" promotional methods, but if you have engaged in some or all of the market assessment needs discussed in Chapter 2, you already have a solid sense of the learners' needs and a good idea of what will maintain interest over time.

A shining example of sparking and sustaining interest is the Rapid E-Learning Blog written by Tom Kuhlmann for Articulate, a maker of tools that help people create sophisticated e-learning experiences starting from PowerPoint. Since its launch in 2007, the Rapid E-Learning Blog has grown to a subscriber base of more than 90,000, fueled by a steady stream of content from Kuhlmann that appeals directly to the interests of e-learning designers and developers. Naturally, an end goal of this stream of high-interest content is to convert at least some of the readers into Articulate customers, but it is very rare that you see Articulate's products actually mentioned on the blog. The type of wisdom Kuhlmann dispenses is of clear use to anyone who might be interested in products like Articulate's, but it is not limited to this audience. Rather, Kuhlmann and Articulate are providing a service to the broader e-learning community with the understanding that, over time, being a center of interest leads to significant returns in the form of sales of its e-learning products.

Motivation

The Rapid E-learning Blog illustrates another essential difference between connecting with learners in their informal networks and simply interrupting them at a random point in time: By choosing the former you are much more likely to meet them where they are motivated, where they actually have the desire to learn. Think of the difference between being told to take a class or read a manual and stumbling upon a problem that sparks your interest and provokes an intense desire to find an answer. The latter is much more likely to engage you because it is a real need attached to a real situation. As noted earlier in this chapter, adult learners, in particular, are motivated by learning that is relevant, that has practical and immediate applications to the issues they are encountering in their life and work. With the power of search, it is now commonplace for someone seeking to solve a problem to turn to Google or a social network like Twitter, Facebook, or LinkedIn. If your content is what comes up in the search results, you have connected at a point of maximum motivation. If your content then helps the searcher solve the problem, guess where that person is likely to turn the next time a problem occurs?

Outcomes

Outcomes, of course, are key. Informal networks provide an opportunity for you to help learners solve problems and get a sense of the larger value you may be able to provide. They provide a context for disseminating evidence of this value. They also provide a context in which "social proof" can be offered by others. Social proof is a psychological phenomenon in which we rely on cues from others to help us make decisions, whether consciously or unconsciously, about our own behavior. In sales- and marketing-oriented situations, it is significantly more powerful for customers and prospective customers to attest to the positive outcomes of a product than for the maker of the product to attest to the same outcomes. This type of proof surfaces constantly and spontaneously across the web. There are entire sites like Yelp and Angie's List that are dedicated to gathering and sharing feedback from customers, but prospects and customers also are constantly talking across networks ranging from Twitter to Facebook to discussion boards and listservers.

There is, of course, a danger in all of this conversation, but it is one that I think high-value, ethical learning providers should welcome. Namely, if you aren't delivering, if you simply aren't providing the promised learning outcomes, this information will surface eventually and could damage your reputation significantly. For providers who are simply out to take the money and run, this may be the end of the road. For providers truly interested in creating value, however, it is an opportunity to engage with the community and correct course.

NOTES

1. Robert F. Mager, *Preparing instructional objectives: A critical tool in the development of effective instruction*, 3rd edition (Atlanta, GA: CEP Press, 1997), p. 45.

2. Ibid.

3. Elwood F. Holton III, Malcolm Knowles, and Richard A. Swanson, *The adult learner: The definitive classic in adult education and human resource development* (Taylor & Francis, Kindle Edition), Chapter 4: A Theory of Adult Learning, "The Andragogical Model."

4. Ibid., Kindle Location 1269. Kindle Edition, Chapter 4: A Theory of Adult Learning, "The Andragogical Model."

5. John Medina, *Brain rules: 12 principles for surviving and thriving at work, home, and school*, (Perseus Books Group, Kindle Edition).

6. Ruth Colvin Clark and Richard Mayer, *E-learning and the science of instruction: Proven guidelines for consumers and designers of multimedia learning*, 2nd edition (San Francisco: Pfeiffer, 2011), p. 66.

7. Holton, Knowles, and Swanson, Kindle Location 1312. Kindle Edition, Chapter 4: A Theory of Adult Learning, "The Andragogical Model."

8. Ibid., Kindle Locations 1273–1275. Kindle Edition, Chapter 4: A Theory of Adult Learning, "The Andragogical Model."

9. Jay Cross, *Informal learning: Rediscovering the natural pathways that inspire innovation and performance* (San Francisco: Pfeiffer, 2007), pp. 243–244.

10. Ibid., pp. 7–8.

11. Daniel H. Pink in Tony Bingham and Marcia Conner, *The New social learning: A guide to transforming organizations through social media* (Alexandria, VA: ASTD Press, 2010), p. xiv.

12. The Nielsen Company, February 16, 2011. Retrieved February 17, 2011, from www.blogpulse.com. At the time this book is being written, there are more than 115 million blogs in existence. This can be substantiated purely by the number of Tumblr blogs (63.7 million, retrieved July 12, 2012, from http://www.tumblr.com/about) and the number of WordPress blogs (53.8 million, retrieved July 12, 2012, from http://en.wordpress.com/stats/), which represent only a subset of the total.

13. Michael Stelzner, "Why major marketers are moving to Google+," *Social Media Examiner*, March 16, 2012, www.socialmediaexaminer.com/why-major-marketers-are-moving-to-google.

14. "Smartphone market hits all-time quarterly high due to seasonal strength and wider variety of offerings, according to IDC," IDC Press Release, February 6, 2012, www.idc.com/getdoc.jsp?containerId=prUS23299912.

15. "Media tablet shipments outpace fourth quarter targets; strong demand for new iPad and other forthcoming products leads to increase in 2012 forecast, according to IDC," IDC Press Release, March 13, 2012, www.idc.com/getdoc.jsp?containerId=prUS23371312.

CHAPTER 6

TOOLS AND COMPETENCIES

AS SHOULD ALREADY BE CLEAR from earlier parts of this book, content is crucial in the new learning landscape. Content is not just—or even mostly—about courses. You need it for formal learning experiences—for example, traditional seminars, online courses, or webinars—but just as important, you need it for the wide range of informal learning interactions you will help create for your customers as well as for marketing.

The range of tools now available for creating, delivering, and managing educational products is truly astounding. Indeed, there are now so many affordable options that it is easy to become overwhelmed. To keep both your sanity and your bottom line intact, your instructional strategies and your business model should be a constant point of reference as you make decisions about the types of products you create. In other words, don't do it—whatever "it" is—just because it can be done and seems to be the latest thing.

In almost everything you do, it will pay to create with an eye toward versioning and repurposing. If, for example, you deliver a classroom-based seminar or a webinar, remember that:

- ◆ Either can be captured as video for reuse as a web or CD/DVD-based product.

- ◆ It may be possible to "chunk" the captured content into multiple segments, each of which might be a separate product.

- ◆ It may be possible to use clips from it as a marketing tool.

- ◆ The audio can be extracted from it and used as a separate product.

- ◆ The audio can be transcribed and mined for articles or shaped into an e-book or, for that matter, a print publication.

- ◆ All of these pieces can be combined, recombined, and repackaged with each other or with pieces from other educational experiences to create different versions of a product—typically aimed at somewhat different audiences—or new products entirely. (Note: As a rule it is always wise to make it clear that you have repurposed content from one medium to another.)

The bottom line is that it pays to view any situation in which you are delivering knowledge or learning as a production event that may be a source for numerous spin-offs.

While it is possible to outsource many if not all of the tasks in the preceding list, I'd argue that it pays to build a reasonable level of hands-on capabilities in content production. Doing so will help ensure you are as agile and flexible as possible when it comes to creating content, and it keeps you tuned in to new possibilities and opportunities. If and when you do outsource, having direct knowledge of key tools and skills also helps greatly with articulating your needs and finding the right help. Ideally, you or someone on your staff should have a least a serviceable level of skill in each of the areas that follow.

MANAGE A HOME BASE

Whatever the nature of your educational offerings, they have to "live" somewhere, and ideally you should have complete control over that somewhere. This doesn't mean you have to own the software and the servers. In fact, in most cases it makes more sense not to have responsibility for maintaining and supporting these parts of the equation. But you *do* need to have complete editorial control, meaning that you can easily post content, change content, modify the look and feel of the site, and, in general, determine what the user experience will be. If you rely purely on third parties that limit your control over these things, or if you always have to rely on assistance from a service provider or a staff member from another department, you are seriously limiting your ability to conduct business effectively in the new learning landscape.

At a minimum, the people in charge of a learning business—whether that means a solo entrepreneur, a training firm, or an education department—need to have access to all relevant parts of their web content and know how to make basic changes to text and graphics. They should also know how to post or link to standard content like video and audio files or documents. They should be capable of doing these things, to the extent they are supported, on any social networking sites or other third-party sites that you use, but keep in mind that users of these sites do not ultimately own or control them. There is no guarantee, for example, that Facebook or Twitter or LinkedIn will be around in their same form in five years, that they will offer the same sort of user experience, or that their policies will remain in line with the goals of your business. As I have already indicated throughout the book, these types of sites can be powerful tools, but ultimately you generate the most value for your business by bringing people back to a home base that you own and control.

In many organizations, this is no small issue. Often the technology and marketing departments are in charge of key resources required for successful implementation of a business model. If this is the case, you may have to work hard to break down silos and gain the rapid, flexible level of collaboration you need, or figure out ways to gain control over your own platform and marketing resources.

A final note about managing a home base: Blogging platforms, and in particular the free WordPress blogging software, have become very powerful as hubs for an overall web presence for learning providers. Blogs started out as a way to publish content frequently and easily, both of which are desirable capabilities for learning providers. Over time, some of them have evolved into sophisticated and yet still relatively easy-to-use content management systems. WordPress, for example, can be used to deploy and manage a multipage website with multiple levels of navigation. A blog is only one component of WordPress sites, and, indeed, the site does not have to contain a blog at all (although I can think of very few circumstances in which it is not desirable for a learning provider to have a blog). Additionally, there are now excellent options for turning WordPress into a membership site as well as adding e-commerce capabilities and various types of collaboration tools and integrating it with popular e-mail marketing platforms and other systems—including the open-source Moodle platform, the most popular learning management system in the world. (There is more about learning management systems later in this chapter.) All of this can be done without any knowledge of programming, but should you want to delve deeper into the possibilities, you will find there are vast armies of freelance programmers who know how to customize WordPress in just about any way imaginable. For learning providers starting from scratch or looking to make a technology switch, I'd argue WordPress is one of the first options that should be considered for core website capabilities.

SHOOT AND EDIT DIGITAL VIDEO

Video is one of the most valuable media available to you, so it makes sense that you should have at least some level of capability for producing it. In many situations, a web camera or the video camera on a smartphone is sufficient for capturing presentations, conducting interviews, or shooting brief promotional pieces, but I think it is also well worth investing in a decent-quality digital video camera. Look for a camera that shoots high-definition video and also supports attaching an external microphone. In order to capture high-quality audio you need to have the flexibility to run a microphone to whomever is speaking, rather than capturing audio from wherever the camera is positioned. Finally, invest in a decent tripod to go with the camera. This one small accessory can dramatically increase the overall quality of your video and also makes it possible for a single presenter, working alone, to capture video.

For editing, the iMovie software that comes standard on Macs is hard to beat for affordability and flexibility. This software alone almost makes it worth ditching your PC. There are, however, some good low-cost options available for PC. Sony, Adobe, and Pinnacle all sell packages under $100, and Corel has recently released a package under $100 that will produce video in HTML5—the standard supported on iPads, which will not play Flash-based video.

Video can be hosted in a number of ways. For free hosting of short clips (up to 15 minutes in length), YouTube is an obvious choice both because of its ease of use and because it is the second-largest search engine in the world. For brief videos that are part of your marketing efforts, there is usually little reason to use anything other than YouTube. For larger video files or files for which you want more than the very basic privacy options supported by YouTube, services like Vimeo and Viddler provide a range of options. At the time I am writing this book, Vimeo offers a free option for uploading up to 500MB of content weekly, but you will need to opt for one of the company's paid plans to upload more and to take advantage of a fuller range of features. Finally, Amazon Web Services offer low-cost, pay-only-for-usage hosting, though taking full advantage of these for hosting and streaming video requires a certain amount of technical skill.

RECORD A SCREENCAST

The ability to record whatever appears on your computer screen and narrate as you do so is known as "screencasting." It is another form of video, but one that deserves to be discussed separately from video captured with a camera. Using this approach, you can quickly demonstrate how to perform basic tasks in a software program or on a website, or you can record yourself presenting a PowerPoint deck, just to name some of the obvious possibilities. Whenever you launch a new offering, screencasting is a great way to do a quick walk-through of highlights. Most screencasting tools also enable you to combine what you capture on the screen with video captured from a camera, so you can easily shift back and forth from a narrator to whatever the narrator is talking about. It's worth pausing for a moment and considering that less than a decade ago you needed a professional studio—or, at the very least, a whole lot of time on your hands—to achieve this level of production.

There are a range of good tools available for screencasting these days. For very short clips, there are even free options like Jing from TechSmith. For longer videos, TechSmith's full-featured product, Camtasia, is one of the more popular choices, along with Adobe's Captivate. Both of these products are available for PC and Mac, though Mac users may also want to consider ScreenFlow (my personal choice). Links to these and other resources related to video and screencasting can be found on the resources site for *Leading the Learning Revolution* at www.learningrevolution.net/tools.

CAPTURE AND EDIT AUDIO

As popular as video is, audio will always remain a powerful medium for learning products if only because learners are often not in a position to actually watch content, but may be still be able to listen to it. Think of the daily commute as just one key example—this is prime time for learning that audio can serve well.

As with video, it is possible to capture audio on a smartphone, tablet, or other digital devices that you may already have. I am an advocate, though, of investing in a small, dedicated digital recorder. Good ones can now be found for well under $100, and a freestanding recorder gives you the option of handing it off to staff member, volunteer, or anyone else who may be helping you without having to give up your device. Regardless, you want to have some easy way to capture audio interviews at conferences and other events where you may encounter people with interesting insights and perspectives.

Additionally, having an easy method for capturing digital audio from phone interviews can be highly valuable. One of the easiest approaches is to subscribe to a phone conferencing service, like FreeConference.com, that enables you to record your conversations and provides an audio file. Using this approach, all of the parties involved in an interview can dial into a conference bridge. The downside to this approach is that each participant's voice is captured in a single audio file, making it more difficult to adjust volume levels or address other variations in voice quality from speaker to speaker. My preference is to use the Internet phone service Skype in combination with call recording software like Call Recorder (for Mac) or Call Burner (for PC). Both of these provide capabilities for capturing separate audio tracks that can then be adjusted and edited independently. This option can work well even if the person you are interviewing does not use Skype. Skype offers an inexpensive "Skype to Phone" service than enables you to call landlines and cell phones around the world. Additionally, if you happen to need to interview someone who insists on calling you, you can set up a phone number that is attached to your Skype account. When the person calls, you answer on your computer and use either of the call recording packages mentioned here to record the call. (Note: For legal and ethical reasons, *always* make sure the person you are recording knows that you are recording the call.)

For recording interviews through a computer or other digital device, you will need a good USB microphone. For phone interviews, a headset microphone is best, and I have found medium-priced models from companies like Logitech to be adequate. For recording panel interviews or other live situations, I recommend the Snowball line of microphones from Blue Microphone.

For editing, Macs are again hard to beat—they come with the Apple's audio production software, GarageBand, already installed. Another great option, though, that works on either Mac or PC, is Audacity, a free open-source audio editing application. With either option, you may also want to consider using The Levelator, a free application (though donations are encouraged) that adjusts the voice levels in an audio file so that they are roughly equal. If you do an interview in which your voice is much louder than that of the person you interview, or vice versa, simply dragging and dropping the file into The Levelator will fix the issue.

In many cases, it makes sense to spruce up audio files a bit and make them feel more professional by adding intro and exit music. GarageBand offers a range of royalty-free music clips you can choose from for this purpose. Other sources include Mevio's Music Alley, where you can find a variety of artists that make their recordings available for free use in a podcast with proper attribution, and Royalty Free Music, where you can purchase large libraries of royalty-free music.

Finally, once you have produced audio, you are going to need a good way to host it. You can, of course, simply upload it to your website and have visitors download it from there, but this can slow down your site, and it may not create the best experience for your users. Sites like Libsyn and Podbean specialize in podcast hosting at relatively low cost. Alternatively, as with video, you can make use of Amazon Web Services.

DO BASIC IMAGE EDITING

If you want to experience the power of simple edits to images, visit the wildly popular website ICanHasCheezburger. Based almost entirely on people applying captions and other minor edits to pictures of kittens and cats, the site has become one of the most popular destinations on the web and has spawned a series of other popular sites. You may not achieve the same impact with your educational content, but clearly a little bit of editing can go a long way! Among the paid options for image editing, Adobe Fireworks is hard to beat as an all-around solution not only for modifying images, but also creating graphics for the web. However, both the learning curve and the price may be more than some learning providers want to swallow. Some good alternatives that are both significantly cheaper and less complex are Paint.Net for PCs (www.getpaint.net; free) and Acorn for Macs (http://flyingmeat.com/acorn; $49.95). Either of these programs provides adequate capabilities for manipulating images and creating original graphics.

HOST A WEBINAR OR WEBCAST

The web is flooded with webcasts and webinars—many of them free—but even so, an ability to use this medium well is among the most essential skills a learning provider can possess. Aside from its usefulness in delivering lecture-type learning experiences, a good presentation/communication platform can be used for:

◆ **Brief product overviews.** A webinar or webcast can be particularly helpful when introducing a new offering. By holding a live event to demonstrate the value of a new course, membership site, conference, or whatever it is you are launching, you have the chance to engage with your existing customers and connect with new ones. It is particularly powerful in these situations to have a satisfied learner from a previous offering talk briefly about the value you or your organization can provide.

◆ **Q & A sessions.** A webinar or webcast can be an excellent medium for delivering question-and-answer sessions related to specific topics covered in your learning offerings. This can be particularly useful when the majority of your content is offered on a self-paced, on-demand basis: A Q & A session gives learners the opportunity to get any pent-up questions answered. Sessions can be offered based on participants submitting their questions live, in real time, or—often a better approach—based on receiving questions ahead of time and addressing them during a live session, accompanied by appropriate visuals to support the answers. Naturally, it can be very valuable to record a session like this and make it available in both audio/video and audio-only versions.

◆ **Discussion groups.** Webinar platforms can also be used for facilitating real-time discussion and interaction among participants in a learning experience, whether through text-based chat, audio chat, or a combination of the two. For a relatively small group, video chat may also be a viable option. The Hangouts feature on Google+ is one of the more recent options for supporting video discussion groups. Skype also offers a similar capability.

◆   **Group coaching.** A variation on discussion and Q &A, webinars can also be great tools for engaging relatively small groups in more intensive learning related to a particular topic or issue. Coaching of this sort can be a particularly useful aspect of the Flipped Model discussed earlier in the book.

WEBINAR VS. WEBCAST VS. PODCAST: WHAT'S THE DIFFERENCE?

web·i·nar \web-uh-nahr \ noun: a live or recorded session that combines audio with presentation text or graphics (e.g., Microsoft PowerPoint)
web·cast \web-kast \ noun: a live or recorded session that combines video with presentation text or graphics (e.g., PowerPoint)
pod·cast \pod-kast \ noun: recorded audio or video without presentation text or graphics; packaged for distribution (e.g., via RSS)

You can no doubt think of other uses for webinars and webcasts based on the specific goals of your business. All of these can be delivered in real time and, when it makes sense, recorded for later replay. There are numerous options available for delivering webinars and webcasts, and you may want to take advantage of different platforms for different purposes. (I discuss these in more detail on the resources site for this book at www.learningrevolution.net/tools.) As a general rule, though, I recommend identifying a single platform that you will use most of the time. To ensure maximum flexibility for both you and your learners, the platform should:

◆   Allow for easily presenting standard document types like PowerPoint and Microsoft Word.

◆   Support both dial-in and voice over Internet (VoIP) as an audio option. (Although it is increasingly common for learners to be familiar with and make use of VoIP, using it alone can still cut into attendance significantly among many audiences. Having dial-in as a backup can be useful when unforeseen technical issues arise.)

◆ Allow for text-based Q & A with participants, and ideally, text-based chat among the participants.

◆ Include the ability for the presenter to broadcast video.

◆ Support recording of the session in a way that gives you full access to the recording file.

Webinars and Webcasts: Rising Above the Fray

To stand out in the crowded webinar space, you have to deliver experiences that won't put learners to sleep (or on multitasking autopilot) and that are also designed to generate maximum value from you as a content producer. Many people these days are quite jaded when it comes to webinars. The standard "show up and throw up" approach does not jibe with more sophisticated learner expectations.

From your standpoint as a learning provider, you want to be able not only to attract people to the live event and deliver a high-value experience, but also to capture the event and reuse it in a variety of ways. Doing this means adhering to many of the same principles discussed in Chapter 5 that will make the event instructionally effective and compelling but also paying attention to seemingly minor details. The following are a few key points to keep in mind.

Distinguish "Inform" and "Perform." Ruth Colvin Clark and Richard E. Mayer define "inform" programs as those that communicate information, while "perform" programs build specific skills.[1] Using this distinction, "inform" webinars—like the typical "subject matter expert shares basic information or news" model so common across the webinar landscape—might be offered at little or no charge to members. These can be positioned as a member benefit and as fulfilling the organization's mission, and in most cases we recommend they carry no credit. "Perform" webinars, on the other hand, should offer a richer experience that might include, for example:

- Clearly stated learning objectives
- Increased interactivity through the use of self-checks, Q & A, real-time chat, and other activities
- Pre- and/or post-session interactions
- Meaningful supporting materials (e.g., job aids, templates)
- Scored assessments
- A trained, expert presenter
- Availability of continuing education credit

Chunk It in 10s. Use the "chunking" approach advocated in Chapter 5. In addition to maintaining learner attention and supporting learning, this approach makes it much easier to pull out segments of the webcast later as freestanding video or audio files.

Segment Question Times. Pause at specific times to engage in question-and-answer rather than answering questions randomly. Like the chunking approach, this will make it much easier to carve out slices of content later.

Provide Pre, Post, and During Materials. Giving attendees the option to download the slides is standard for webinars and webcasts, but the practice is of limited value. Often slides don't hold up well on their own, and having to sift through them to find links or other items referenced during a presentation can be an annoyance for attendees. Provide the slides if you want to, but also provide at least one other user-friendly, high-value piece of content to accompany the webinar. This might consist of an article, or a link to an article, to read ahead of time; some questions for the attendee to consider before, during, or after the event; a list of valuable links related to the event content; or worksheets or other aids to help the attendee actually implement concepts covered in the webinar.

Establish a Consistent Look and Feel. Create (or have a designer create) a standard, professional template for your webinars. This will provide consistency of experience across your events and also make it possible to piece together segments from multiple events while maintaining a polished appearance.

Record the Webinar in Multiple Ways. While you can typically use editing tools to separate out video and audio, I find that it is often easier—and the quality is often better—if you capture a separate voice file of your webinar or webcast. This can then be easily converted into an audio-only podcast or used for transcription. Also, consider using a simple digital video camera to capture yourself delivering the event. This can be used for "action" footage in promoting the event or may even provide for some great nuggets of content to present independently of the full event.

Keep It Timeless. Make sure you (or any presenters you use) avoid time-based expressions like "Good morning!" or references to the date or day of the week when you are presenting. If the content has lasting value, there is no reason to date it in the learner's mind by providing unnecessary information about when it was recorded.

CREATE NICELY FORMATTED DOCUMENTS

Finally, don't underestimate the power of making the various documents you present or provide to learners look as professional as possible. This rule applies even to handouts, worksheets, and other "utility" documents. Indeed, because these documents are often shared, and because so few providers take the time to make them look as good as they could, a little extra effort can go a long way.

You don't have to be a graphic artist to make things look professional. Just spend a bit of time learning how to use basic features like styles and headers and footers in Microsoft Word or Apple Pages, for example. This is also one area where most providers can benefit from some outsourcing: Use Elance or another freelance service to find someone to set up some nicely formatted, branded templates for you in Word, PowerPoint, or other types of documents that you use consistently, and then *use these templates consistently* when creating new documents. Again, this helps to create a polished appearance in all of the materials you present.

Additionally, convert your documents to PDF whenever providing them to customers or prospects, unless part of the value you are providing is the ability for the documents to be modified. The PDF format can provide some protection for your intellectual property—though I think worrying too much about this kind of protection is a losing game—but, more important, it preserves your formatting and branding as documents are viewed on different computers and different platforms.

MORE SOPHISTICATED TOOLS

Discussing the available tools is a bit like pulling a thread on a sweater, but there are two other categories of tools that deserve careful attention, particularly from providers who plan to offer credit for and/or track performance in learning experiences.

Rapid Course Creation Tools

Mastery of highly sophisticated online course authoring may not make sense for individual subject matter experts or smaller organizations. If there is a reason for investing in this type of production, it probably makes sense to outsource it to a firm that specializes in online course development. Over the past decade, however, tools that can produce nicely structured, trackable learning experiences based on Microsoft PowerPoint have really taken off. The power of these tools lies in the fact that most computer users, and business users in particular, have at least some level of comfort with PowerPoint. Articulate's Rapid E-Learning Studio, Adobe's Presenter, and TechSmith's Camtasia are among the leading software packages in this category. Additionally, Articulate has released a new rapid authoring tool set, Storyline, which publishes to HTML5. Each of these takes a slightly different approach to enabling conversion of PowerPoint-based content into a form that can be installed into a learning management system that will then track a learner's progress through completion of the material. To varying degrees, these tools also allow for insertion of different types of interactivity into a course, from basic knowledge checks, to assessments, to learning exercises and games.

Learning to use one of these tools at a basic to intermediate level is well within the reach of most subject matter experts. Rapid course creation tools often make a great deal of sense for creating on-demand experiences based on existing lecture and seminar content, particularly because PowerPoint slides often already exist for these formats. Even if you don't plan to use a learning management system, the ease with which these types of tools enable you to organize content, provide a navigation structure, and attach accompanying files such as job aids and tip sheets make them well worth considering.

Let's say that you're a subject matter expert and you're thinking, "I've got all this great knowledge. I can take it online. I can build a business around this. I'm going to make some e-learning courses." What are the key skills or knowledge you need to make a good course? I asked this question of Tom Kuhlmann, author of the wildly successful Rapid E-Learning Blog.

The first step, Tom suggested, is to understand whether or not it really needs to be a "course." "If you're just having them read screens of information," he noted, "then maybe a PDF is a better solution than authoring a course." While arguably there is not really much difference between reading text on a PDF and reading text in a course, people bring different expectations to a course.

Once you have determined that a course is really the right approach, Tom sees visual design as perhaps the most necessary skill for developing courses that stand out. He emphasized that, while instruction is an important part of visual design—the visuals need to support the other content in an appropriate way—emotion is equally important. "E-learning is mostly a visual medium," he said, "and people are drawn to those things that look good and make them feel good. There's an emotional connection to what they're doing. They like to click things. They like to roll their mouse over buttons and move things around. That's an important part."

Finally, Tom noted that simply making the effort to be consistent visually, to "make your buttons look like buttons" and make everything "look like it all belongs to the same course" can go a long way toward creating a polished, effective learning experience.

Get the full interview with Tom Kuhlmann at www.learning -revolution.net/podcast/.

Learning Management Systems

In many areas of adult learning, students participate based on their own motivations and have their own view of what the outcomes should be. In these cases, there may not be a need for tracking participation and performance. There are, however, many other cases in which knowledge of student participation and/or performance is essential for managing the issuance of continuing education credit, tracking advancement toward a certification, or ensuring compliance with regulations and policies. Or you may want to maintain a closer connection between learning content and related activities like discussions, assignments, or assessments, which can easily be achieved with less specialized software. In these cases, using a learning management system (LMS)—software that is specifically designed for capturing learning data—may be necessary.

A basic LMS will typically enable you to:

- Present a catalog of courses
- Enroll learners
- Launch courses
- Track learner participation and completion
- Test learners in a basic way
- Generate reports

More advanced systems may also support:

◆ Basic content authoring

◆ Webinar/webcast capabilities

◆ Classroom management

◆ Collaboration/social tools

◆ Sophisticated assessment

◆ Credit and certification management

◆ Competency management

◆ E-commerce

◆ Integration (e.g., with a customer relationship management system [CRM] or an association management system [AMS])

In the past, the world of learning management systems has been confusing and expensive. While it is still quite easy to get confused and spend a lot of money, the good news is that there is an increasing number of relatively low-cost, straightforward learning management solutions that offer a full range of features. Most of these are hosted by the software provider, which means you do not need to worry about supporting servers but still have a significant level of control over the learner experience. Additionally, there are a number of open-source options that do not require any licensing fees. Indeed, it is the growth of the most popular of these, Moodle, that has helped drive down prices and spark innovation across the LMS industry.

If you decide you need the capabilities offered by an LMS, there are a number of key questions to keep in mind when selecting one. Some of these key questions include those that follow.

What are the e-commerce options? Some of the systems offer shopping cart capabilities that allow learners to select items from a catalog and then go through an e-commerce transaction to pay for them. If the LMS does not offer this option, it has to integrate with other shopping cart systems. What are those systems, and what kind of track record does the LMS have with them? In either case, do the e-commerce capabilities support the kinds of transaction you will require? For example, can it provide for member discounts or bundling of courses for a discount?

How sophisticated are the credit options? One of the key reasons to opt for using an LMS is to be able to track and issue credit. You will want to be sure the LMS can handle the credit scenarios that are important to you and your learners. For example, can multiple types of credit be awarded for a course? A nurse may want one type of credit for a course, while a social worker may want another. Is it possible to require completion of an evaluation before credit is issued? Will the system automatically generate a certificate reflecting the right type of credit? How customizable is the certificate? You get the idea. Think through your credit scenarios carefully, and get the vendor to show you each one in action.

What are the integration options? It's rare that an LMS will not need to communicate with other systems. At a minimum, you will likely want it to integrate with your customer or membership management system. How easily can "single sign-on" between these systems be achieved? Once a user has signed into one of these systems, it should not be necessary to sign into the other; the two systems should handle this invisibly in the background. Can key data from the LMS—like the fact that a learner has earned certain credit—be easily transferred back to the LMS? As already mentioned, is e-commerce integration available?

Keep in mind that the kind of data an LMS tracks may have not only educational, but also strategic value. Knowing, for example, that learners rarely complete a certain course is a clue that maybe you should spend some time talking with learners from the course about the reason. Does the course itself need to be improved? Are learners coming to the course with insufficient prior knowledge—a data point that may suggest opportunities for other offerings? In general, with an LMS in place, you open up opportunities for business intelligence that goes beyond what you may be able to get from less specialized software. So, even if you are not offering content that needs to be tracked for compliance or credit reasons, an LMS may be worth considering.

How portable is the content? You *must* get a clear answer to this question. Once you get content into an LMS you want to be able to get as much of it back out as you can, in case you decide you need a different platform. For any content developed outside of the LMS, this should not really be an issue—and this in itself is a strong argument for relying as little as possible on tools within the LMS for developing content. To the extent that you *do* rely on tools within the LMS for content development, be sure that the LMS conforms to the Sharable Content Object Reference Model, or SCORM, a collection of standards that help to ensure that content can be moved from one system to another and still work properly. Remember, however, that SCORM portability really applies only to structured learning "objects" like lessons. It does not account for other types of content like page text and images that might be part of your learning environment or discussion board threads. Make sure you have an understanding of how this type of content can be gotten out of the system in a form that would make it possible to at least access it later, if not import it into a new system. Similarly, make sure you know how learner data like course enrollments, course completions, credit earned, and other important historical information can be exported from the system.

For additional resources related to LMS selection, see www.learning -revolution.net/lms.

SOURCING AND OUTSOURCING

While I began this chapter with the idea that you need to possess— whether yourself or within your organization—a basic set of skills related to content creation and management, I'd like to close by stressing that this is by no means an argument that you should do all of the work related to producing content. Having a working knowledge of what is involved is highly valuable because of the speed and flexibility it affords.

It is also valuable because it helps you identify and manage other resources for getting the work done.

One key source of content that has evolved over the past several years is a range of sites that are available for licensing photos, images, video, audio clips, and other types of content for you to use in a variety of ways. Some of these require fees; others make content available under the Creative Commons models, which allows free use of content under specified conditions. Some key sources for licensed content include the following:

- **iStockPhoto:** www.istockphoto.com

  Photos, images, and video clips with licenses starting at two dollars per image.

- **Flickr Creative Commons:** www.flickr.com/creativecommons

  Photos and images made available by users of the popular Flickr photo sharing service.

- **Music Alley from Mevio** www.musicalley.com

  Royalty-free music from a variety of artists to use in podcasts and videos.

In addition to to the ability to license content, it is now easier than ever to find qualified contractors to perform content-related tasks, from basic transcription services to more sophisticated programming and course production. Online services like Elance (www.elance.com) and oDesk (www.odesk.com) enable you to search for qualified contractors, post projects for which you need help, and manage the relationship with whatever contractor you hire, including tracking time on the job and handling payment safely. To help ensure the quality of your selection, these services also feature ratings for prospective contractors, information about work history, and scores on various types of skills assessments. As with any hiring situation, there is no guarantee you will find the perfect individual or company, but the odds are certainly higher and the process a whole lot easier than it is with the traditional approach of simply posting an ad. I have had very good success with finding help for research, editing, transcription, and a variety of other services using these platforms.

For outsourcing needs related specifically to development of educational content and online courses, I also recommend searching the Buyers Guide on the eLearning Guild website (www.elearningguild.com/buyers_guide) and potentially posting to the job board there (www.elearningguild.com/job_board/jobs).

NOTES

1. Ruth Colvin Clark and Richard E. Mayer, *e-Learning and the science of instruction* (San Francisco: Pfeiffer, 2008), p. 17.

CHAPTER 7

CULTIVATING THE CONTENT-CONTEXT HABIT

IF LEARNING IS INDEED LIFELONG and you want to attract and maintain customer relationships that span as much of the adult learner's life as possible, focusing solely on individual courses or events is hardly the most strategic way to engage with your market. As discussed earlier in the book, your prospects and customers engage in learning in a variety of different ways day in and day out, and only a small slice of this activity includes participating in formal learning experiences. Ideally, you need to remain a visible, recognized source of value even in the gaps that naturally fall between the times when a learner engages with you formally by, for example, purchasing a course. Creating content to fill these gaps is one of the major uses of the tools covered in Chapter 6. Over time, engaging consistently in producing and distributing valuable free content ensures that you become an important part of the broader context of learning for your audience. You remain top of mind, and as a result, significantly increase the chances that when a formal learning need arises, you will be the obvious choice. Additionally, by producing and distributing content on a regular basis, you remain tuned in to market needs and opportunities and naturally create assets on which your future offerings can be based.

Framed in this way, the business of learning becomes less about specific tools or products and more about consistent habits and incremental steps that contribute to the larger context you are trying to weave. Where are you helping your learners to go over time? How can you continue to add to your value continuum in ways that help to get them there? Again and again I have seen that the individuals and organizations that build a strong audience have done it by continually producing content over time, but doing it toward a long-term vision. Some key approaches to doing this are:

- Staying tuned in
- Curating value
- Conducting rapid research
- Interviewing
- Writing it together

STAYING TUNED IN

A key first step is to embrace the idea that the listening process I described way back when you were assessing your audience in Chapter 2 should never really stop. I encouraged you to set up a dashboard because you want to make this process as easy as possible. With a dashboard, you have a place to tune in to each morning and perhaps at various points throughout the day, much as you would tune in to a favorite radio station. (Remember, RSS is the radio frequency of the Internet!) This doesn't mean you have to read everything that comes through your dashboard. Simply scan headlines and if anything interesting jumps out, click to go deeper. In my own dashboard, I have the various feeds I receive organized into topical categories. I don't track these categories every day, but if I'm focused on a particular category on a particular day, this makes it easy to see if anything of interest has been said recently. I also have certain feeds organized into "Essential Reads" and "Frequent Reads" categories. As the names suggest, these are items I check often.

Another tool I have come to rely on is Zite, a free "personal magazine" software available on iPad, iPhone, and Android. Zite leverages your Google Reader and Twitter accounts to compare your interests with the thousands of articles it scans across the web. The magazine becomes even more personalized over time as you indicate whether or not you like the articles it serves up. It can be a great tool for continually homing in on the best sources for a small set of topics. Every time you launch Zite, the range of resources it presents becomes more and more relevant.

Finally, while special tools like Zite or an RSS reader dashboard are very helpful, the real key is to always have a "discovery" mindset. Whether reviewing your e-mail in-box or flipping through a magazine, keep an eye out for ideas and content to share. As you come across items that may be of interest to your audience, or that may spark ideas for future content development, you might want to mark them for future reference. You can do this in several ways:

◆ **Bookmark** them with a tool like the social bookmarking tool Delicious. This has the advantage of making the links to them accessible anywhere there is a web connection.

◆ **Save them for later** with a tool like Instapaper or Read It Later. These applications save the entire text of any articles you choose in a central location so you can easily access them later.

◆ **Note** them using a tool like Evernote that will sync across all of your digital devices. Evernote makes it possible not only to jot down notes, but also to grab clippings from web pages or even record audio notes.

◆ **Tag** them. Tools like Google Reader as well as most e-mail programs have different ways you can assign "tags" to items so that you can easily search for and find related items later.

◆ **File** them. This works both online and offline. In your e-mail programs and in the file system in your computer, create one or more folders where you save items for future reference. For items you grab from print sources, keep a manila folder on your desk or scan them and put them with the other digital items on your computer.

However you go about tracking things, be sure to set a regular time— preferably at least once a week—to review what you have collected and determine what you will do with it.

CURATING VALUE

Staying tuned in is one step in a process for leveraging content produced by others. An effective way to complement your efforts and deliver value continually to your prospects and customers is to serve as a "curator" not only of your own content, but also of content created by others. The idea behind curators and content curation is that there is such a flood of new content pouring through the Internet pipes these days that being aware of all of it and sorting it out in meaningful ways are simply not possible for the average person. Curators are people or organizations that do the valuable work of sifting through the content within specific focus areas and pulling out the things that seem to make most sense.

There are a number of good reasons why producers of educational material should embrace this approach. Among them are the following:

◆　It provides a valuable service to your prospects and customers and helps to establish and maintain your position as a trusted source.

◆　It can be used to supplement and complement the learning experiences you provide and, as a result, elevate the perceived and actual value of those experiences.

◆　It keeps you tightly connected to learning and knowledge needs in your market and is likely to spark ideas for new products or enhancements to existing products.

◆　It nearly always leads to building relationships that will be valuable to your ongoing business. Through the ongoing process of curation you may develop marketing allies, distribution channels, sources for intellectual property, or joint venture partners.

Curation, I should stress, involves significantly more than finding and regurgitating links. A good curator must be skilled at:

- Locating and evaluating valuable content
- Organizing and connecting content so that it is as accessible as possible
- Creating and repurposing content when it adds to the underlying value
- Capitalizing on the social web to build connections and context
- Building trusted relationships with learners and other curators
- Weaving together learning experiences from the curated content

Bottom line: A curator is an individual or organization that excels at helping others make sense. Again, that is an incredibly valuable proposition in our information-flooded world.

Curating can play a number of roles in your overall product strategy. First, as already suggested, it can help you fill out your Accelerant Curve (see Chapter 4)—particularly at the upper left—by providing content you can link to, comment on, quote from, and otherwise make use of in developing blog posts and articles or simply posting to social media channels like Twitter, LinkedIn, and Facebook. While some readers may worry that pointing to other content will lead prospects away from your own offerings, what you gain in being perceived as a trusted adviser and a source of valuable, filtered information will far outweigh any risk you may incur by pointing your prospects and customers to other content sources. Moreover, you will almost certainly turn people off if your communications are always "me, me, me" in nature—an observation that leads well into a second benefit of curation: It helps you connect with your target community and play a meaningful role.

One of the biggest challenges that producers of knowledge and learning products face is establishing a visible, credible presence in their target markets. Without this presence, the chances of succeeding with even the best of products declines dramatically. As a curator, you can provide a valuable service to a community of interested individuals, and by serving that community well, build up the trust and credibility that will support your future success. I should stress that this rarely works as a mercenary sort of activity. Effective content curation requires time and effort, and you are unlikely to persist at it for very long—or reap the rewards—if you do not genuinely enjoy topics on which you focus and feel motivated to share your own learning.

Part of the process of serving the community, of course, is that you will build relationships with individuals within it. Many of these will be prospective buyers of your products or customers to whom you can provide additional, ongoing value. Some may be potential marketing partners, distributors, or even joint venture partners for developing future products. If you are even the least bit open to it, I can guarantee that you will start and grow a variety of valuable relationships in the process of curating content.

Finally, the process of curation keeps you tapped into your market and will almost certainly provide ideas for new products or for enhancing current products. It is an extension of and much more active form of the "listening" process described in Chapter 2.

CONDUCTING RAPID RESEARCH

Tuning in and curating are very powerful approaches to providing ongoing value to your audience, but you shouldn't rely solely on content created by others for delivering value. Ideally, you need to provide at least some value that is seen as, if not original to you, then at least *originating* from you. One of the most straightforward ways to do this is to conduct some basic research to turn up overlooked information, forgotten ideas, and new perspectives. This doesn't mean you have to be a Ph.D. researcher conducting randomized experiments and statistically valid surveys (though more power to you if you are in a position to do this). A great deal of value can be found simply by putting a little effort into:

- Investigating primary sources
- Conducting informal surveys and polls
- Interviewing experts

Primary Sources

We live in a world of secondhand information. Books cite studies. Blogs cite books that cite the studies. Tweets fly across the Internet with truncated and twisted forms of the original idea. I think people are very rarely out to mislead or distort, but it happens all the time. This is a persistent challenge of the hyperconnected world in which we live, and it is also an opportunity for those who lead learning within a particular field or industry. One of the most straightforward ways to capitalize on this opportunity is to go to the primary sources. Find that original study. Find the research report or the tables of survey data or whatever the source is, and check the facts.

Following the trail to primary sources leads to opportunities to clarify and correct—and thus bolster your own authority—but just as important, it often leads to new areas of investigation. Not so long ago, for example, I read Dan Pink's bestselling book *Drive*, which popularized a number of established ideas about what motivates human beings. In the book, Pink mentions the work of Edmund Deci, a psychologist who has done a great deal of research on motivation in general, and in particular on ideas like autonomy and competence—two concepts that factor heavily into Pink's book. Deci's work led me to the even earlier work on competence by Robert White. This, in turn, led me to begin writing about the concept of competence on my Mission to Learn blog as well as in other projects. This is a simple example, but it illustrates the way in which a little bit of effort can spark creativity when it comes to producing content that is not simply me quoting Dan Pink, as countless bloggers have done at this point.

To get at sources that go beyond what may be easily found in a standard web search, you might want to take advantage of some resources that are readily available, but often not used to the extent they could be. Just using these will put you ahead of many who rely totally on second- and thirdhand information:

♦   The **electronic resources section of public libraries** are perhaps one of the most overlooked research sources. Libraries subscribe to databases on all kinds of subjects. You need a library card to log in, but you can often use your card credentials remotely to get access to many research databases from home, including JSTOR, Gale business databases, and newspaper archives, among other sources.

♦   On **association or governmental websites** look for "Publications" or "Research" in the menu. If an organization does any type of research, it will usually have its stats listed in one of those two places.

♦   Try **Google Scholar** to search professional journals and academic sources. It's just like regular Google except that it only searches academic sources.

♦   **LexisNexis** is an amazing database that covers all manner of legal statutes, cases, public records, and law journals, plus extensive business records and newspapers (even local ones). This is a fee-based service not available from libraries. You need to set up an account and pay monthly, yearly, or "per use" fee (as of this writing, a one-year subscription is eighty-five dollars).

♦   **ipl2** (www.ipl.org), which describes itself as the "first public library of and for the Internet community" is run by library schools and features "pathfinders" or collections of curated resources for lots of subjects. You can also click "Ask a Librarian" and send an e-mail question to which a librarian will respond with three or more relevant, free sources related to your question.

With these kinds of tools, you should quickly be able to get to the heart of just about any topic of interest to your audience and use this knowledge to create content in a variety of ways.

Surveys

Aside from tracking primary resources, *creating* some primary research is another valuable strategy. Conducting surveys to engage with your market and provide some original content—mainly in the form of data collected in the survey—is hardly a new idea. It is still a worthwhile idea, however, because it is so rarely done well.

There are at least two very good reasons to go directly to your market to gather input. One of these was covered in Chapter 2: Direct input from your market helps you to identify needs and serve them in the best possible way. The other is that connecting directly with your market enables you to collect data that others may not have and also to gather stories, examples, and case studies. While it is relatively common for organizations to run surveys or use other forms of research as a way of building their e-mail lists and getting some exposure, it is much less common for the research to be done in a truly thoughtful, methodical way and then be mined for the greatest possible benefits. With a bit of effort, research data can be organized, analyzed, and then presented back to the target market in a variety of forms ranging from a report, an eBook, an informational video, a webinar presentation, or even as part of a formal course. These end products can help establish you as the source and authority for core information in your market. For organizations like trade and professional associations, which are often "brokers" for the authority of others, surveys and other forms of primary research are a valuable approach for focusing the perception of authority back on the organization.

Survey Tips: Achieving a High-Quality "Good Enough." In a perfect world, all surveys would be administered to randomly selected, representative members of a well-defined population. In the real world, this ideal often is not achievable for any number of reasons, including time and budget constraints and difficulties with accurately defining, or "framing," the target population. In these situations, it may still be both desirable and valuable to run "nonprobability" surveys that are not based upon valid statistical sampling. Indeed, you probably encounter the results of such surveys on a regular basis and may have even participated in or run some yourself. The problem with these types of surveys has less to do with their statistical validity and more with how they are presented and used. Most important, their findings should not be generalized to a population broader that the group that actually participated in the survey. Despite that significant caveat, however, they can be very useful tools for collecting clues about a market and for sparking discussion, debate, and new ideas. Ultimately, pinpointing and quantifying human behavior is an elusive goal—even research of the best design and execution will be imperfect in the majority of cases. If you can provide some good points of reference and insights that help your audience and do it with a methodology that is clear and rational, you have performed a valuable service. Some tips for generating as much value as possible:

◆   Even if you are not doing random sampling—for example, if you are running a volunteer survey—it is always preferable to define your audience as tightly as you can and, if possible, control distribution of the survey. That is, determine who will actually receive a link to it, rather than posting a link to which anyone can respond. Online survey tools like SurveyMonkey now offer services for distributing your survey to a targeted list.

◆   Set clear goals for the survey. What question, or questions, should you clearly be able to answer once the survey is done? Clear goals will help you eliminate any questions that do not really relate to the goal and keep the survey as short as possible.

◆   Determine what quantitative data (i.e., numbers, percentages) will be of most interest to your prospective audience. For example, there is perennial human interest in the answers to questions like these:

- How many others are doing what I am doing?
- What are others like me planning to do?
- What kind of success are they having (or not)?

Remember that a key reason for running a survey, at least as discussed here, is to create content that is of value to your audience. What does your audience really want to know?

◆ Don't shy away from open-ended questions. While these can be more difficult to analyze, they often provide insights that would be very difficult to get from quantitative questions, and quoting from open-ended responses brings color to your discussion of results. Additionally, tools like SurveyMonkey now provide basic text analysis as a feature, making it easier to discover key terms your respondents are using.

◆ Use a survey as a way to identify candidates for interviews. Always ask if participants are willing to be contacted for a brief follow-up conversation, and then use the demographics you collect as part of the survey to select a good mix of interviewees.

◆ Pretty much all of the reputable online survey tools provide capabilities for filtering and "cross-tabbing" data. Learning how to use these tools at a basic level is not terribly difficult, and the additional insights you gather can add significantly to the value of the report you ultimately generate from the survey.

◆ Finally, be prepared to report on survey results soon after running it. Use the goals and target data points you defined up front to structure a concise presentation of your findings and make frequent use of visual aids—which many survey tools will generate for you based on the data you select—to help your readers "see" the data.

For much more detail on how to create and administer high-quality surveys, I recommend *How to Conduct Your Own Survey* by Priscilla Salant and Don Dillman. And keep in mind that once you have developed, run, and reported on a survey, you have a template for doing the same survey and report again at regular interviews, thus providing perennial, anticipated content for your audience.

INTERVIEWING

Conducting interviews is one of my personal favorites as a way of developing content. It's a practice that tends to have value no matter what stage you are in or what position you hold in your market. If you are an established expert, conducting interviews is a way of engaging in conversation with peers and being a thought leader in your market. On the other hand, when you are just starting out as a learning provider you may have solid content knowledge but still have a need to build name recognition and authority in your target market. Interviews can help you leverage the authority of others. Finally, you may have discovered a market that you feel has significant potential, but in which you have no real expertise or authority. Again, by initiating and participating in conversations with experts, you benefit from being associated with them.

In each of these cases, interviews can provide a path to establishing authority and developing valuable content. You can use interviews as a way to gather examples and case studies that are of value to your target audience or to discuss issues and trends with experts, just to name a couple of examples. The end product may be audio recordings that you make available as a podcast series or on a CD, print transcripts, article or blog posts based on the interviews, or any number of other possibilities and combinations. In each case, you or your organization are in the forefront and benefit not only from producing the content, but also from your association with it.

One key to the interview approach is to find people to interview who are clearly experts, who have great case studies and examples to offer on their topic, and who will be enthusiastic about discussing it with you. Among the most obvious candidates are book authors, who are always looking for ways to promote their books. People who are active practitioners or consultants in their field are also good candidates. While in some cases these people may compete with you to a certain extent, I have generally found that the benefits from forming a relationship with other experts and providing valuable information to the market far outweigh any competitive factors.

Another key, of course, is to conduct interviews in a way that actually results in useful content. Here are some tips for doing that:

◆ As with surveys, set clear goals for the interview. What is it that your audience is going to find interesting about this person? What specific questions do you want to be sure are addressed? Write these out ahead of time. In my experience, it is difficult to cover more than half a dozen questions in twenty to thirty minutes—a typical length for a podcast.

◆ Do your homework. Make sure you know the major highlights of the interviewee's past experience and accomplishments. As appropriate, dig deeper in the specific areas that are likely to be of interest to your audience so that you can reference these during the interview. This is not only common courtesy, but it also helps to establish credibility and a level of comfort with the interviewee. Consider asking the interviewee ahead of time if there are specific questions he or she would like you to ask.

◆ Finally, listen. It's easy when conducting an interview to always be thinking ahead to the next question. If you do this, you may miss opportunities to take the interview in interesting and unexpected—but highly valuable—directions. Additionally, interviewees often know when you are not fully engaged in the discussion and hold back, whether consciously or unconsciously, on their answers.

As simple and straightforward as the tips are, it is well worth reviewing them frequently and making sure you are actually practicing them as you engage in conducting interviews.

Long before writing this book, one of my inspirations for pursuing interviews with experts was Michael Stelzner, whose Social Media Success Summit was discussed in Chapter 3. I asked Stelzner to share his perspective on how to get real value from doing expert interviews. Here's what he said:

The first thing you have to do is acknowledge that experts have certain insight in their minds that is complementary to what you think. Say you're an expert in social media. There are many other experts in that space and they all have a unique perspective, depending on what their background is. Acknowledging that these folks have some unique insight in their mind is the first step in establishing a relationship with them.

The next thing you want to do is to know how you can leverage something that's in the mind of these experts and use it to produce value to your audience, and this can be as simple as doing an interview with them at your event, doing a podcast with them as we are doing right now, or interviewing them about a new product or book they have out. By doing that you've accomplished a number of things. One, you've shared some unique insight to help provide great content to your audience. But you've also given that expert something they find valuable, which may be either exposure to your audience or recognition for some of the things they have accomplished. By doing that you can help build a pretty powerful following.

In the case of *Social Media Examiner,* when we launched, interviews were instrumental to our success. We took a camera crew with us to a trade show called Blog World and we interviewed almost two thousand individuals from different backgrounds. They were about ten-minute videos, and a lot of these people were extremely well known. Sharing this video with their audiences helped us to grow a major following at the beginning of our launch.

WRITING IT TOGETHER

You may have noticed a current running though the content habits I have already discussed: Each of them typically requires a certain amount of writing, even if only to introduce and frame the content that comes out of them. Even when you are dealing with audio and video content, a certain amount of text is inevitable if you want to convey meaning effectively and—not a trivial point—be found by search engines. Moreover, text is almost always required to make connections between all of the various types of content you produce, from formal learning experiences like courses to less formal content like blog posts or tweets. In short, there is probably no greater asset, no greater skill to have in the context of the new learning landscape than to be able to write reasonably well and to do it regularly.

For some readers, I know this will be a daunting thought. Being an effective presenter or someone who knows how to organize educational events does not, of course, in any way guarantee that you will be comfortable as a writer. But if you look around, the people and organizations that are dominating markets these days almost always excel in writing, whether this means writing excellent copy (it nearly always means this), providing a stream of informative articles, blogging regularly, or even tweeting in a way that is actually effective. Writing content brings knowledge; writing brings connection; and knowledge and connection are power. Bottom line: You or someone in your organization needs to be reasonably capable of writing well and writing on a consistent basis.

Fortunately, this does not mean that you need an Ernest Hemingway or a Jane Austen on your side. The key, as the title of this chapter suggests, is to establish a habit and then develop it over time. The following sections provide some tips for establishing a writing habit.

Put It on Your Calendar. Let's start with the glaringly obvious: If you don't schedule time for it, it won't happen. Block out some amount of time on your calendar daily to do some writing. Ideally, allow for at least thirty minutes; it's generally pretty difficult to get into the flow of it and produce any substantial amount of content in less time than this. And make sure this scheduled time is actual writing time. Not research and reading time, not organizing time, but time to put words on screen or paper with the goal of creating something of value for your audience. Even if you sit there for 30 minutes and write next to nothing, keep at it. Over time, your mind will adjust to seeing that time as a time to produce content.

Read (and Watch, and Listen) Both Narrow and Wide. It is next to impossible to write in isolation. Reading what others are writing helps you continue to build expertise, find new ideas and perspectives, and absorb knowledge about how to write effectively. Make it a habit to read regularly what your primary "curators" are writing about (there's that whole "listening" thing again!), but don't let yourself develop tunnel vision. Read outside of your areas of expertise and across a variety of formats—books, blogs, magazines, even Twitter feeds. Watch videos. Listen to podcasts. And don't limit yourself to nonfiction—often reading fiction or poetry can provide you with some of the most interesting perspectives.

List, Organize, and Target. As noted, one of the key reasons to read is to spark ideas and creatively borrow concepts that you can make your own. Our working memory only stores so much at one time, however, so if you expect to be able to return to and flesh out that great idea later, you had better write it down. As you do this over time, you will almost certainly start to see patterns emerge in the type of things you are writing about. (And, of course, you will also be using the listening methods covered in Chapter 2 to track what seems to be resonating with your audience.) As this happens, organize your writing efforts into major topical areas, and start laying out and maintaining an editorial calendar. Whether this is for a blog, a book, a series of videos you want to produce, or anything else, laying out a clear plan and deadlines for all of the items on the plan marks a move toward being serious about creating content on a regular basis.

Write What's Easy First. Part of what makes any habit enjoyable—thus increasing the chances you will stick with it—is to build an initial sense of competence. Don't approach writing with the idea that you have to tackle complex and difficult topics or produce the next great treatise on the human condition. Look to areas in which you feel truly familiar and fluent and begin from there. And beware the "curse of knowledge," the common affliction that makes us feel everyone must know what we know. They don't. Write about basic principles in your field, for example. There are any number of novices on any given day who will welcome your insights because they really *don't* know what you know.

Revisit and Revamp. As I noted in the earlier chapter on "Learning by Design," repetition is fundamental to learning—and that happens to be a very good thing for you as a writer. People need to hear things over and over again, framed in different ways, to truly absorb them. Once you have written about a topic, you have a great prompt for writing about it again in the future. Return to what you have written on a regular basis and see if there are updates, additions, or new perspectives you can offer. Many of your prospects or customers won't ever have seen what you wrote earlier, and even if they have, don't worry about it. If you are ever concerned that similar messages can be repeated too often, just peruse the magazines in the checkout aisle at your local supermarket. Week after week, month after month, you see the same sorts of stories—and yet people keep coming back for more. Remember, too, that things you have written before can be adapted to new formats—one or more blog posts may provide the basis for a SlideShare.net presentation, a video, an e-book, or even a full-blown book, among other possibilities.

FROM BLOG TO BOOK—AND BACK

One highly productive way to use a blog is as a way to draft a cohesive longer work over time—essentially, to write a book. While most people are daunted by the idea of writing a book, producing smaller amounts of content is usually manageable. A blog gives you an easy way to produce and organize small amounts of content so they can ultimately be organized into a book. At the same time, having a vision for a book can help tremendously in coming up with topics to blog about on a consistent basis.

The trick is to start with a relatively clear roadmap to guide your writing. Whether you already have a blog or are starting a new one, take the time to map out major themes and related subthemes you would like to cover over time. You don't have to write in the precise order in which you might present content in a book—that level of organization can come later—but your roadmap should help you stay within the general focus of your desired end product. (Even if you have no plans to publish an actual book, this is often a much more productive way to blog than simply throwing up random posts as they occur to you.)

Depending on how prolific you (or your team) are as a writer, it may take anywhere from months to more than a year for the content to add up to a book, but, regardless, you wind up with a fairly cohesive body of knowledge that can be a true asset in your efforts to create knowledge and education products. Aside from being shaped into a book, content developed in this way can be packaged into articles, used as the basis for scripting a formal course, or converted into audio recordings.

Books and other products developed from blog posts are very often good vehicles for driving traffic back to your website and directing people to the range of educational products and services you offer. For a selection of writers who have successfully leveraged blogging to produce a book as well as tools to help you with the process, visit www.learning-revolution/blog2book.

CHAPTER 8

PROMOTING AND CONVERTING

IF YOU ENGAGED in the type of market assessment covered in Chapter 2, you essentially baked marketing in from the beginning. You looked to your customers and prospective customers to provide input on their needs, and you developed your product accordingly. To do this, you had to get a sense of the terms your prospects might use to find your products through searching on the web—and that work will now help you with using search to market your product effectively. You also listened in on social networks and may have already built some new relationships and discovered who some of the major influences in your markets are. Those efforts will serve you well as you now continue to build your networks and deepen your relationships. Finally, as part of your testing process, you have already begun to develop a list of prospects you can contact through e-mail and, if appropriate, direct "snail" mail. This list is one of your most valuable assets. Let's take a look now at how to leverage these earlier efforts and convert prospects into customers for your knowledge and education products.

FROM ATTENTION TO ACTION

The principles that apply to promoting products in the new learning landscape are not fundamentally different from those for promoting products in other new markets or, for that matter, in the old educational marketplace. You have to be able to catch the eye or ear of your prospect and ultimately persuade that person to try whatever it is you have to offer. Not coincidentally, the elements of successful marketing are also very similar to the four points I articulated for engaging successfully in informal learning environments (see Chapter 5). The underlying reason for this, of course, is that both marketing and learning are fundamentally about human behavior, and the two disciplines draw upon many of the same underlying principles. If you are an excellent teacher, I'd argue, you have the makings of an excellent marketer, and vice versa. Recognizing the connection is essential in a world where learning and marketing share many of the same communication platforms and technologies.

The framework I used in discussing informal learning was an adaptation of the classic Attention, Interest, Desire, and Action, or AIDA, advertising model first suggested more than 100 years ago by advertising pioneer E. St. Elmo Lewis. I revisit it in its original form here from the perspective of promoting your educational offerings.

Attract Attention

You have to gain a prospect's attention before you will have any hope of actually getting her to do something. In today's world, with the constant barrage of new information flowing through the web, mobile devices, television, and numerous other communications channels, that's harder than ever. As bestselling author and marketing guru Seth Godin has put it, your offerings have to stand out like a "purple cow" among a field of brown cows to actually catch the prospect's eye. Fundamentally, this means your products must offer exceptional value, but they must also project exceptional value to the prospect if you expect anyone to care.

When thinking about how to attract attention, put yourself in the mind of your target prospect. There are a hundred other e-mails in her inbox. She regularly receives postcards and brochures from your competitors. What is the "headline" that is going to spark her interest? A good headline (the subject line in an e-mail) often asks a provocative question—"Is your professional development putting your members to sleep?"—or promises clear, concrete value—"7 Quick Compliance Tune-Ups That Your Firm Can Implement Today."

Ideally, a great headline will be complemented with an image to help to make it more powerful and concrete—a photo of a classroom full of snoozing learners, for example, to go with the first headline I just mentioned. Many organizations, I find, create generic campaigns in which the headline is along the lines of "Knowledge You Can Afford" and the image is of something like a piggy bank. They look professional and polished, but there is really nothing in them that would attract a prospect's attention. The headline may as well be "Put me in the recycling bin immediately."

Maintain Interest

Attention is important, but once you have it, at least a hint of significant value needs to be right there with it if you actually expect to hold someone's attention.

Question headlines are great because they imply that you are going to provide an answer to the question. Similarly, when your headline suggests that you will provide a list (e.g., "5 Quick Tips for . . .) or "how-to's," the reader is almost certain to be interested in finding out what the list items or the how-to's are. The answers to these questions can then point to the even deeper value that will be delivered through your educational programming.

Notice what that means? The promotional materials themselves must provide some level of value. They are not simply fluff. They are not simply a decorative path to a registration form. As I've suggested throughout the book, this is an increasingly important point in today's highly competitive education markets: Every time you put yourself in front of prospects, you should be delivering at least some small bit of value. Even if you don't ultimately gain a registration, you will have helped to sustain general interest in your organization and its overall value.

Create Desire

Interest is valuable, but on its own it usually will not lead to action. You must help the prospect connect interest with need and conclude that your solution is the right fit. Good promotions have a sort of "layered" impact. You grab attention, you spark interest with both the promise and the initial delivery of value, and then you keep the value—and promise of even more value—coming.

I've already pointed to one key aspect of creating desire: actually providing answers, tips, and other types of value in your promotional materials. Another key tool, and one that few organizations use as well as they could, is "social proof" in the form of testimonials. Include quotes from actual learners, including their names and preferably with photographs, talking about the results they achieved from participating in your educational offerings. If you can get video of this, so much the better.

"Results," I should add, goes beyond the listing of "benefits" that appear in much promotional literature. You want outcomes, return on investment, cause and effect. "Because I went to this education program I can now do X, Y, and Z." "As a direct result of what I learned from this seminar, my company has increased sales by 15 percent this quarter." You get the picture. You are aiming for that treasured "I gotta get me some of this!" response.

Get Action

In the world of religion, preaching is nice, but conversion is everything. (At least it is down in the South, where I live.) The same is true in marketing. You can grab their attention and get them all lathered up, but if they don't ultimately click "buy" or "subscribe" or "get the full story" or "like" or whatever it is you want them to do, you are putting in an awful lot of effort for very little return. This applies doubly or triply if you don't have actual salespeople who can ask for the sale. So what is the key to an effective call to action? In a nutshell: Ask them for the right thing at the right time.

Let's start with simply "ask them." I routinely encounter marketing materials that have a phone number in tiny print on the last page, or a "click here" link buried three clicks in to a promotion. As calls to action, these are almost worthless. A prospect should never have to search for or decipher a call to action (i.e., If I "click here," what's in it for me?"). In most cases, the "ask" should be made multiple times in a promotion, and the result the prospect's action will lead to should always be clear.

Also be sure that you ask them the right thing. That may not mean "buy now." As suggested by the first three elements of marketing discussed in this section, effective promotion is a process of establishing value. Depending on what you are selling, and to whom, there may be multiple stages, and as a result, multiple actions that prospects need to go through.

If the only "ask" you ever offer your education customers is for them to register—i.e., fork over some money—whenever they receive a seminar or conference promotion from you, don't be surprised if they aren't exactly eager to hear from you.

TOOLS OF THE TRADE

There are now so many ways to communicate with prospects and customers that you could devote all of your time to trying to understand and use them all. It's very tempting to try the latest widget, network, or formula with the hope that this one will do the trick, but over time it has become clear that focusing on a few key tools and learning to use them well will get you the highest-quality, most consistent results. The tools are e-mail, search, a limited set of social media applications, video, and effective landing pages, which support the first four tools in this list.

E-Mail

Given all of the attention that social media and cutting-edge technologies have gotten over the past few years, you might think e-mail communication is not as important as it used to be. In fact, quite the opposite is true: A high-quality e-mail list is perhaps the most valuable tool you have for effectively promoting your educational products. Pay attention to highly successful Internet marketers and you will notice almost unanimous agreement on this point. More important, you will notice that all of them put a great deal of effort into cultivating and managing high-quality lists.

The two key characteristics of "high quality" are:

1. Every person on the list has *requested* inclusion on the list and confirmed the subscription. In other words, you didn't buy the list from some third party or simply add people to your database without their permission.

2. People on the list have signed up because they are interested specifically in your educational products. In other words, you didn't attract them with something else with the hope of interesting them in your products.

If these two factors are true, then an e-mail list is typically head and shoulders above other means of communication. Having specifically asked to hear from you, recipients are much more likely to pay at least a little bit of attention to what you put in their inboxes. That little bit of attention can be invaluable. I have found in numerous interviews with trade and professional association members, for example, that most are highly reactive when it comes to choosing what they will do for continuing education. Rather than methodically planning out the courses they will take in a given year, they often go with whatever sounds good along the way. If you are able to put valuable options in front of them with some regularity, the chances that you will get their business—rather than having it go to a competitor—go up significantly. You can and should use other promotional channels, but the combination of permission and immediacy that e-mail offers is hard to beat.

In addition to ensuring that your list is built on clear permission and interest from your subscribers, you need to be sure that messages will actually make it to your subscribers' inboxes rather than getting trapped in a spam filter somewhere along the way. The most direct approach to doing this is to use an e-mail marketing service provider—often referred to as an "autoresponder" that adheres to strong antispam standards and has a good reputation for "deliverability." You can check deliverability ratings using services like these:

- www.senderbase.org/index
- http://reputationauthority.org/index.php
- https://www.senderscore.org/

Another key advantage of using an established e-mail service provider is that you will have the ability to track major data like click-through rates and will have access to tools for segmenting your list and testing the effectiveness of different versions of e-mails you send out.

Building the List

If you have been following the advice in Chapter 2, you have already been building an e-mail list. The key now is to not ever stop. Here are some key practices for driving your list-building efforts.

Ask, Ask, Ask: This one may seem obvious, but often it is *not* obvious that a learning provider has any sort of newsletter or other e-mail list or where to sign up for it. Ideally, an e-mail list sign-up form should be a persistent part of your website, preferably in the top left quadrant, where visitors' eyes are likely to go first when landing on a site. The form or a link to the form should also be just about anywhere else you can put it, including in your e-mail signature and in any print campaigns you send out. In all cases, the "ask" needs to be permission driven. Rather than your adding them to the list yourself, prospects should go through the process of signing up and then confirming that they want to be on the list. This is a process any good autoresponder can support, and it will be a great help in ensuring the quality of your list.

Value First: One of the most important keys to retaining list members and attracting new list members is to provide value consistently *before* making any sort of promotional offers or otherwise soliciting business. There are two reasons for doing this. The first—discussed throughout this book, particularly in Chapters 2 and 4—is that you are much more likely to keep people's interest and build a long-term relationship with them if you are helping them rather than overtly selling to them. The second is that a list that focuses primarily on special offers, discounts, and other promotional tactics is likely to mostly attract people interested in those things—which, of course, contributes to downward price pressure and general devaluation of your offerings over time. Share tips and insights that your list members can't easily get elsewhere. Make sure these are relevant to whatever promotions you may include in the e-mail and you will accomplish the double goal of providing value while also helping to ensure that your offers stick in the minds of your list members.

Target the Value: All good e-mail list services provide ways to segment parts of your list based on list member characteristics such as job title, past purchases, or self-selected interest areas. By using these capabilities, you can send communications about a particular topic or issue only to those list members who are most likely to care about it and pay attention. This helps increase the perception of your relevance for these recipients and cuts down on other list members feeling overloaded with e-mails that don't pertain to them.

Keep a Conversational Mindset: Your e-mail list is a great place to leverage the listening you have been doing through other channels and, as noted earlier in the book, is a key avenue for asking customers for their perspectives. As you see new issues and opportunities emerging, use your e-mails as an opportunity to provide tips and insights on these and also to solicit list member perspectives through polls and surveys. The responses you receive are, of course, great material to share in future newsletters and can help drive your ongoing product strategy efforts.

Connect It with Other Media: E-mail is an important bridge to the other types of media you use. If you ask or answer a question on e-mail, point your list members to one of your key social media locations to discuss and get additional resources. This is one of the key uses for a blog. Blogging is an easy way to post additional content related to your e-mails and to provide a place for e-mail list members to comment. Note that by using services like FeedBlitz and AWeber, you can easily integrate your blog with e-mail list capabilities. I find that an increasing number of experienced Internet marketers have started making their e-mail lists an extension of their blogs. Instead of running a separate e-mail list and blog, each new broadcast to the e-mail list is essentially a way to bring people back to a marketer's website via valuable information published on the blog. When done successfully, this increases contact with prospects, boosts the time that list members spend on the marketer's website, and ups the chances that list members will make a purchase or take some other desired action. (One true expert at this is Derek Halpern on the Social Triggers blog: http://www.socialtriggers.com.)

Yet Again, Test: You have probably noticed by this point that I am an advocate of testing different options and versions of things to see what really works. Few platforms are better than e-mail for this. All good autoresponders provide the ability to send out two or more versions of an e-mail to your list. You may, for example, send out the same e-mail, but with two slightly different subject lines, to a subset of your list to see which one gets opened and clicked on more. You then send out the one that performs the best to the broader list. Depending on the size of your list, even a small percentage difference between one e-mail version and another can make significant difference in the results you ultimately achieve.

Track and Learn: As the previous point suggests, good e-mail list services give you the ability to see who is opening your e-mails and what they click on. By tying these actions into tools like Google Analytics on your website, you can follow them all the way through purchase, sign-up, or any other action you want your list members to take. Naturally, this gives you an amazing amount of visibility into what is working and what isn't with your e-mail communications. For this information to matter, though, you have to first pay attention to it and then actually learn from it and make adjustments. By persistently tracking and fine-tuning over time, you can develop a fairly solid idea of what is going to happen just about any time an e-mail is sent out.

SEARCH

In Chapter 2 we saw how useful search tools can be for assessing your overall market. Search is also essential as a tool for promoting your products. In markets where there is a reasonable level of demand, it is almost certain that a significant portion of your prospects will find you by using Google or another search engine. You need to be as sure as you can that when they search on terms that relate to your offerings, you will come up at or near the top of the search results.

SEO Basics

Because search engines—and Google in particular—frequently change the algorithms they use to find and present search results, search engine optimization is always something of a moving target. Even so, the fundamentals that follow in this section have not varied a great deal for years. If after you apply these you find that search traffic turns out to be one of your better sources for leads, consider also working with a reputable search engine optimization consultant.

Keywords. As discussed in Chapter 2, these are the words—most typically phrases—that you might expect web searchers to type in when seeking out the types of products and services you offer. For instance, "diabetes management online training" might be an appropriate keyword phrase for a page where an online course in diabetes management is sold. Thinking through these phrases from your prospective customers' perspective is extremely helpful when assessing your market, and it is also important for shaping the content of the pages on your website. While Google and other engines don't rely upon keywords to nearly the degree they once did, the bottom line is that if your site does not contain the keywords your prospective customers are searching on, you will not rank in the search engines for those keywords, and, as a result, you may not be found. So, make sure the landing pages for your offerings contain the keyword phrases your prospects are likely to be searching on. If you have done the searching and listening work covered in Chapter 2, you know what these are. Don't overdo it though; just include them as a natural part of the content on any page. If you do otherwise, the search engines may think you are "stuffing" your pages and ding you in the rankings as a result.

Title Tags. There is a great deal that is beyond your immediate control when it comes to ranking high in the search engines, but along with using keywords effectively, how you title your web pages does have some impact on search engine results. This has remained true for years, in spite of the many changes that have impacted—and sometimes eliminated—other aspects of optimization.

Most of us don't tend to pay a lot of attention to the bit of text that appears at the top of our browser window on each web page we visit, but Google and other search engines do. These are called page titles, and pretty much any web editing software or content management system provides a field for you to say what this title will be. The page title is one of the key places where you want to use the most important keyword phrases you have identified for the page. On my site Mission to Learn, for example, I have a page that offers a definition of learning.

www.missiontolearn.com/2009/05/definition-of-learning

One of my goals is for anyone who happens to be searching for a definition of the term "learning" to find that page. So, in my page title, you will see the phrases "Definition of Learning," "Define Learning," and "What is Learning."

The effectiveness of the page title can be enhanced by using the most important phrase in the title in the top-level heading for the page as well as in the URL for the page. In the Mission to Learn example, "Definition of Learning" is a top-level, or H1, heading for the page; the web address, or URL, of the page contains "definition-of-learning."

Currently this page ranks number three in Google results for "definition of learning," right behind two entries from the venerable Merriam-Webster dictionary. While it would be a mistake to think that this ranking was achieved purely as a result of the title tag, heading, and URL, these elements have clearly played a role.

These aspects of search engine optimization—the ones that you can control and edit on your own web pages—are referred to as "on-page" elements. One last on-page element worth mentioning is the "meta" description you provide for each page. This is the brief bit of text—160 characters on Google—that appears below your page title when search engine results are generated and that, ideally, give the searcher some additional information about what can be found on the web page if she decides to click through. While this text does not appear to be taken directly into account for ranking purposes by most search engines, it is important for making the value of your page clear to the searcher, thus increasing the chances of a click-through. If you don't specify what this text will be by typing it into the field provided in your web editing software or content management system the search engine will typically grab the first lines of text from your web page and use those. These may or may not be optimal. In the Mission to Learn example, the meta description that appears in search results is:

Here's a concise definition of learning used to guide writing about lifelong learning on Mission to Learn.

This is different from the initial text that appears on the actual web page, but from my perspective, is more in line with responding to the question a searcher is likely asking: Where can I find a good, concise definition of "learning"? It also makes clear that I offer this definition in the context of writing about lifelong learning, thus increasing the chances that anyone who clicks through may have some interest in this topic.

External Linking. While "on-page" elements like keywords and tags are important for search engine ranking, they are not nearly as important as a range of elements over which you have less direct, if any, control. One of the most important of these is the number and quality of links to a page from pages on other websites. A good tool for determining both number and quality is Open Site Explorer at www.opensiteexplorer.org. The basic version of Open Site Explorer is free, while more advanced options are available for a monthly subscription fee. (You can also search on "link:www.yoursitename.com"—without the quotation marks—in Google, but I find the information provided by Open Site Explorer to be both more useful and more user-friendly.)

There are various aspects to link quality, but in general, you want any links to a page in your site to come from web pages with similar, related content. The pages should also have as high a ranking in the search engines as possible. In other words, it is more valuable to get a link from a page that turns up number one in the search engine results for keywords similar to yours than from one that shows up on page ten of the search engine results. It also helps if the "root domain" of the linking site—that is, the URL you would type in to get to the main page of the site (e.g., www.sitename.com)—is very popular. In the case of Mission to Learn, for example, one of the sites that links to the Definition of Learning post is The Open University (www.open.ac.uk), which is a very popular, high-authority site. That link alone is probably one of the key reasons that my Definition of Learning post ranks as highly as it does in the search engine results.

Finally, it is also helpful if the text used for links to one of your pages—the actual words the user clicks on—contain some variation of your keywords. So, for example, when other sites link to my post on the definition of learning, I don't want them to use a link with text such "click here" or "see what Jeff Cobb as to say." I'd much rather they use text along the lines of "here's a good definition of learning." Indeed, this is important enough that it is worth specifying the language you want other sites to use if you ask them for a link.

Asking is, indeed, one way to go if you want to ensure that you are receiving links from relevant sites. Asking for links from a lot of different sites can be time consuming, however, and many site owners or web masters will simply ignore you if they have no idea who you are. If you are going to ask, it is best to focus on a handful of highly relevant, high-traffic sites and build a relationship with the right person at those sites prior to asking. However, the best strategy overall for attracting links from other sites is simply to publish content that is valuable to your market on a regular basis.

Internal Linking. In addition to showing external links to your site, Open Site Explorer tool will show which other pages on your site link to the page on which you are running a search. These links are important from the perspective of Google and other search engines. Generally speaking, every page on your site should be linked to at least one other page on your site.

Finally, you should make sure your key landing pages are linked as many times as reasonable from other pages. "Reasonable" means following rules similar to those discussed in the previous section for external links. You want to connect pages that are highly relevant to each other. For example, if you mention your diabetes course in a blog posting or a newsletter article about diabetes somewhere on your site, it makes perfect sense to make sure that some of the text in which the course is mentioned is hot-linked to the page in your catalog that contains the course. Your aim is to create a sort of "web of relevancy" throughout your site that helps the search engines find and value things appropriately.

Paid Search

On the surface, paid search services like Google AdWords and Microsoft adCenter may seem like one of the best deals going. As noted in Chapter 2, the way they work is that you identify keyword phrases that you think your prospective customers will type into a search engine. When they actually do type in these phrases—or variations of them, depending on how you set things up—an ad for your product will appear either off to the right side of the browser window or, in some cases, across the top, whenever the search results are returned. The best part is that in most cases, you don't pay a dime unless the searcher actually clicks on your ad. Sounds wonderful, but as you might expect, there are challenges.

The first is one that we have already encountered as part of the market research discussion in Chapter 2; namely, you are not the only one who would like to put ads in front of prospects. Paid search works as an auction, and depending on your market, you may have many competitors willing to outbid you to show up on page one of search results. There are factors aside from the price you pay per click that affect how well your ad performs, and unless you either invest time to understand all of these factors or pay an expert to run your ad campaigns, you can end up wasting a lot of money very quickly on paid search. For a short run of initial market research spending money to attract clicks can be seen as an investment worth making, but obviously you don't want to overspend on ads over the long haul.

The other issue with paid advertising is that once you stop paying, both your ads and the traffic they produced are gone. No traffic, no sales. In nearly all cases you are much better off putting time into building up "organic" traffic that is based on providing great content and paying attention to the search engine optimization fundamentals discussed in the SEO Basics sections of this chapter. Use paid search for initial market research, to jumpstart traffic when you launch a product, and possibly on a conservative basis over time to supplement your efforts to build traffic organically. For in-depth information on how to use AdWords specifically, I would again highly recommend the third edition of *Google AdWords for Dummies*.

SOCIAL TOOLS

Earlier in this book (in Chapter 3 and Chapter 5) I discussed how social networks, blogs, and other social media are an integral part of informal learning as well as how they can be leveraged to enhance formal learning experiences. More often than not, when social tools are used successfully for learning purposes they also serve implicitly for marketing. When social media is really humming, it will organically achieve what our e-mail and search efforts achieve through our concerted efforts and do it in the best way possible—customers talking to other customers and prospects. Learning is one of the best catalysts there is for these sorts of conversations.

Given the way in which learning and marketing connect organically through social interaction, it is tempting to not even call out social media as a distinct marketing tool. It is, in a sense, integrated into how the business of learning is conceived in this book. Nonetheless, it pays to think of social media in explicit marketing terms when promoting your products if only so you can develop clear tactics for directing social interaction toward business results. Put another way, social media activity needs to convert into more business over time if it is to truly count as a marketing tool. There are essentially five key ways it can do this:

1. By building your brand. As already discussed, brand matters greatly in the new learning landscape. A strong, distinctive brand can practically eliminate any desire your prospect has to look at competing providers and is one of the single biggest factors in maintaining your price points. Social media is a particularly powerful tool for branding because it leverages the principle of "social proof," the idea that we are all susceptible to going along with what others like us are doing. The concept of "listening," covered in Chapter 2, is particularly important both to tracking and to measuring the impact of social media branding efforts. However, before you begin really trying to leverage social media as a marketing tool, you need to know your starting point. How often is your name or information about your offerings being tweeted, posted to Facebook or LinkedIn, or otherwise shared? Use listening tools to establish a baseline for these metrics, and then track how and whether they increase over time as you start engaging more with social tools.

2. By generating traffic. Just about everything on the web can be measured, and this includes whether your efforts in social media are actually bringing people back to your website. If you don't already have Google Analytics (http://www.google.com/analytics) installed on your website, put that at the top of your to-do list today. It's free, and it can be implemented even by people with a relatively low level of technical ability. Google Analytics will tell you the sources of clicks to your website, including whether they come from LinkedIn, Twitter, Facebook, or any other social site.

3. By providing actionable market intelligence. At this point in the book, I'm hoping I hardly need to cover this one. Clearly there is a variety of ways that social media can be leveraged to learn more about your market in general as well as about which of your specific efforts are having the most impact—indeed, each of the previous two points illustrated some of these capabilities. I find that many providers feel if they are not able to see a clear link trail from social media to purchases of their products and services, their social media efforts are of questionable value. Don't underestimate, however, the value of the market knowledge that social media can provide. It may provide just the edge you need to break clear of your competition and really connect with your market needs.

4. By generating leads. This is the area in which social media doubters are likely to become believers. Once again, if something happens on the web, the chances that it can be tracked are very high, and this applies to your lead generation efforts. In the first place, you can put things like sign-up links and in some cases even purchase links directly on many social media sites. AWeber, for example, is among a number of e-mail list providers that provide the ability for e-mail sign-up forms to be put on a Facebook page. You can then directly track whoever uses this form to sign up for your e-mail list. If you direct users back to your site from a social media site, you can follow them through to the point of conversion by using—you guessed it—Google Analytics. Google Analytics enables you to set "Goals" on your site—like having users sign up for a newsletter, download a specific document, or purchase a product—and then track individual users from the source of entry into your website through the completion of that goal.

5. By cultivating loyalty. For my money, this last one may really be the most important. In a world that is so flooded with information and points of connection with other people, finding the places and people that really help you make sense of things is invaluable. Social media does not, of course, magically make that happen, but as I have suggested throughout the book, it is a powerful tool for helping you establish the sense of context and community so essential to building lifelong relationships with your lifelong learning customers. How important this is was suggested by a study the American Society of Association Executives did in 2009. The study, called The Decision to Learn, explored why it is that members of trade and professional associations decide to participate in education offered by these organizations as opposed to the myriad other choices they may have. Far and away the biggest reason was a sense of "affiliation." Basically, when people feel that an association represents "their people," they are much more inclined to participate in the association's educational offerings.[1] This sense of belonging is of particular importance in the world of membership organizations, but I have not the slightest doubt that it also extends into the broader world of business. We all tend to gravitate toward businesses and other organizations with which we feel a sense of affiliation, and as choices multiply, this becomes even truer. Social media platforms offer significant potential for simply being human—connecting with and communicating with your prospects and customers, and facilitating their connections with each other.

Which tools you should use for any of these goals should be determined by what you have discovered through your ongoing listening activities. Specifically, where are your prospective customers most active? Focus on the one or two networks they use most, and unless you have resources to spare, dedicate no more time to other networks than it takes to set up a complete profile. It's better to fully engage in one or two place than to simply dabble across many.

VIDEO

In talking about market assessment in Chapter 2 I mentioned that YouTube, the video-sharing site owned by Google, is now the second most used search engine. This fact alone suggests how important video has become as part of the overall landscape of the web. Its importance specifically as a marketing tool is also significant. *Social Media Examiner*'s 2012 Social Media Marketing Industry Report indicates that "76% of marketers plan on increasing their use of YouTube and video marketing, making it the top area marketers will invest in for 2012."

As a marketing tool, video is clearly an important medium for delivering high-value content that helps build relationships with prospects and customers over time. By providing sample and demonstration content through video, or content that simply extends, enhances, or otherwise complements the content in your paid offerings, you make it clear to prospects and customers that you are a trustworthy and valuable source of knowledge. "How-to" content, in particular, is highly likely to be shared. Some readers may recall, for example, that when the initial buzz was starting to build around social media, a two-person company called Common Craft released a series of entertaining and educational videos explaining key social media tools and concepts "in plain English." These were wildly popular and were shared millions of times across the web. You may not experience such dramatic results, but even more modest results make video well worth the effort.

In addition to helping build exposure for you and your offerings, video can help to put a human face on your business—meaning both your face and the face of your customers. Video is particularly powerful for capturing testimonials from satisfied members or customers: Social proof is stronger when prospects can both see and hear the person giving it.

CONVERTING WITH LANDING PAGES

I touched on landing pages in Chapter 2. In the context of that chapter, a landing page was a place for testing potential products. Once you have validated demand and created your products, you once again need landing pages for actually selling these products. In this case, a landing page is what many learning providers think of as a description page for a particular course in their catalog. It's the place where, ideally, you should be communicating the *value* of a product and *converting* a prospective buyer into an actual buyer.

A landing page is where the action is when it comes to selling products online. It's usually the last place a visitor "lands" on your site before clicking the "Buy" button, and often it is the first place as well. If a user finds a particular course offering through a Google search, for instance, she may go straight to the page on your site that has information about that course—i.e., the *landing page* for that course—and never see anything else on the site. The stakes are high; you need to get that user to click "Buy," or take whatever other action you have determined, while she's on that page or you may lose her forever. So how do you achieve that goal? Here are ten tips for making sure your landing pages convert prospects into buyers:

1. Use concise, benefit-driven headlines: A good landing page will have a heading at the beginning of it—i.e., large, bold text—that gives the visitor an idea of what she will find on the page. Don't just use the title of a course for this: State concisely a major benefit the visitor will receive from the course. What burning problem will you help the prospect solve? What important goal will you help her achieve? Speak to what you feel your prospective learners care most about.

2. Put the important stuff "above the fold": "Above the fold" simply means the area of the screen that most people see in their browser without having to scroll. (This term, which originally referred to the top half of the front page of a newspaper—i.e., above where the newspaper is folded—has been co-opted as a common term in web page design.) People tend to focus on what is at the beginning of a page and, to a lesser extent, what is at the end; they are likely to skim most of the rest. If you offer credit or some other form of validation for the course, make sure that is obvious. A testimonial and picture above the fold can also be highly valuable (see #6 in this list).

3. Have a clear call to action: A "call to action" is simply your request that the visitor do something. Initially this may mean signing up for a list or downloading a document, but eventually it means clicking a "Buy" button (or whatever language you use) to make a purchase.

Whether the call to action is above the fold or farther down will vary according to factors like the complexity of the product, price of the product, and how users arrive on the page (i.e., did they get there from an advertisement on another site or on a search engine, or are they coming from another page in your site?). In general, the more costly and more complex the product and the less the visitor knows about you, the more likely the call to action will need to be farther down the page, appearing after you have provided the visitor with compelling reasons to take action. You should also repeat it at least once on the page (generally at the end), and perhaps more than once, depending on how long your copy is.

4. Lead with a strong value proposition: I find that many organizations simply launch into a description of course content at the beginning of their landing pages. It is important, of course, to have good content, but a potential purchaser cares much more about the value she will derive from the content. Again, what problem does it help the prospect solve? What new doors will it open? Once you have captured the prospect's attention, carry through with a strong headline and build a strong case for the value you will provide.

5. Focus on the buyer: You are great. Your organization is great. However, those are secondary considerations for the buyer. She wants to know that you understand her situation and have created something that really meets her needs. Write your landing page copy in the second person: Forget "we" and "I" and focus on "you."

6. Provide social proof: One of the best ways to convey the value of an offering to a buyer is to provide testimonials from past buyers with whom she can identify. If you are not in the practice of gathering testimonials from people who participate in your learning offerings, start today, and start putting a high-quality testimonial above the fold on each of your landing pages.

7. Include pictures of people: Pictures are a good thing in general on landing pages. In the case of online learning products, which may prompt some prospects to worry about lack of communication with an instructor or other learners, pictures of people can be reassuring. When possible, try to get pictures of the actual customers who give you testimonials. Be sure to put captions on your pictures that identify and reinforce the types of benefits the people in them have received from your offerings.

8. Use subheadings: I noted in the second point in this list that visitors to a page will generally skim most of the content that appears below the fold. Using subheadings—larger, bold text—to call attention to key areas of your copy throughout the page can help ensure that points that do not merit a place above the fold will be noticed. In general, your landing pages should be very easy to scan, and every heading should lead logically to your call to action.

9. Don't send visitors away for more information: The only reason visitors should leave a landing page is to take the action you want them to take. If you feel you have to provide additional information that might make the page copy too long, do it by using pop-ups or rollovers.

10. Keep it simple and focused: This rule applies first and foremost to the call to action. Don't list five different pricing scenarios with a "Buy" link for each scenario. Use a single "Buy" button, or possibly a member and nonmember button if this is relevant to your organization. If you *really* have to offer more pricing scenarios than that (*and think long and hard about whether you really do!*), then do it on a second page that appears after the "Buy" button on the initial landing page has been clicked. In general, keep your language simple throughout the text on the landing page, and don't present the visitor with extraneous options. Your landing page should have one and only one goal—to get the user to take the desired action. To the greatest extent possible, anything that interferes with that should be removed.

If you follow these rules you should end up with a strong landing page, but don't take my word for it: *Always test your landing page.* One of the easiest ways to do this is to use the A/B split testing that is available at no cost using Google Website Optimizer. The basic approach is to create a copy of your original landing page and then make one (and only one) significant change to it—for example, changing the headline or changing the image that appears above the fold. Website Optimizer will then automatically alternate the pages on a visitor-by-visitor basis and track whether visitors complete your call to action. (This is tracked by whether the visitor ultimately ends up on the page you present once the call to action is completed—a thank you page or an order summary page, for example.) By tracking in this way, you can see if one version of the landing page leads to more conversions than the other and eventually switch to using only that page, or continuing to test it against additional versions. Small changes in landing pages can dramatically impact how well they convert prospects to buyers, so it is well worth doing at least some testing each time you create a landing page. Full details on Google Website Optimizer, including detailed "how-to" instructions, can be found at www.google.com/websiteoptimizer.

NOTES

1. Lillie Albert and Monica Dignam, *The decision to learn: Why people seek continuing education and how membership organizations can meet learners' needs* (Washington, DC: Association Management Press, 2009).

CHAPTER 9

THE BEST LAID PLANS: EXECUTING, MEASURING, INNOVATING

AN ISSUE THAT PEOPLE in any line of business face is that it is often easy to generate ideas and create plans, but putting those ideas and plans to work and consistently executing over time is another matter entirely. This problem is often compounded in times when technology is changing rapidly and there is a persistent temptation to try the latest tool or fear that a better tool will come along as soon as you decide to go with the current best option. Success may not be quite as easy as "just showing up," as Woody Allen put it, but there is a lot of value to the notion that simply doing *something* on a consistent basis will get you a lot farther than sitting around talking about what you want to do or waiting for the next new thing. In this chapter we'll discuss how to develop a mindset that will get you out of the starting gate and ensure that you are not only a learning provider, but also an organization that learns (even if you happen to be an organization of one).

THE BETA MENTALITY

One of the key barriers that most learning providers must overcome initially is the idea that they have to produce the perfect product or experience right out of the gate. This barrier is often stronger when multiple people are involved, as it is easier to defer decision-making responsibility and delay action. In the world of knowledge and learning, however, there is almost never a "perfect" product. Knowledge evolves, often at a rapid pace, and even if you are dealing with a perennial topic that does not change very fast, methods of instruction or delivery are almost certain to change. For that matter, external factors like the economy and the competition never stand still. That means delays in the name of perfection are almost never warranted.

Learning providers these days can benefit from embracing the sort of "always in beta" mentality that search engine giant Google espouses for its products. As the company's official comments put it, "We believe beta has a different meaning when applied to applications on the web, where people expect continual improvements in a product. On the web, you don't have to wait for the next version to be on the shelf or an update to become available. Improvements are rolled out as they're developed." This line of thinking goes double for knowledge and learning products that are delivered or enhanced by the web—which encompasses nearly every type of product covered in this book. Get the product out there and then immediately begin working on improvements, additions, extensions, and other ways to keep the experience fresh and relevant. Aside from freeing you to get off the mark and put products into the market quickly, the beta mentality assures that you will stay in continual dialogue with your customers and better know how to provide the content and experiences they will most value.

It should be stressed that the beta mentality is not an excuse for shipping junk. I introduced the idea of a "minimum viable product" in Chapter 2, and the "viable" part of this idea must be taken seriously. Whatever is rolled out initially *must* meet some set of core needs and the information it conveys *must* be accurate. Just as important, the process of learning that is inherent in the beta mentality must be pursued with discipline. You must be prepared not only to gather data about the use of your offerings and solicit input from your learners, but also to put all of this information into action in driving future development.

As Scott Anthony of Innosight put it in a recent *Harvard Business Review* blog post on the concept of the minimum viable product,

> "Good enough" is a great way to start the innovation journey because it enables learning in the most important laboratory of all—the marketplace. But it's hard to build a compelling business with something that's just barely adequate. Customers might be intrigued enough to try it once, but they won't come back.

Of course, if you have been engaging with your prospective audience in the ways advocated throughout this book, there should not be much danger of putting out an offering that is "barely adequate." You should be well positioned to put out products that are viable and then evolve rapidly from there.

In my travels in the trade and association world I have met few people who embrace the "beta mentality" with the vigor of Lloyd Tucker, deputy executive director of the Society for Technical Communication. Lloyd has consistently created and managed e-learning initiatives that have contributed significantly to his organization's revenue. I asked Lloyd to provide his perspective on the concept. Here is his response:

Motivational speakers often say, "be bold, be fearless." In my opinion, not enough people are paying attention to this advice. If your job is to provide education in support of your profession, then you need to do just that, not talk it to death. I cringe every time I hear someone say, "It took us a year to select a learning management system." Waiting for a perfect system or solution leaves you always waiting. I rarely meet resistance from a board of directors or an association membership when I provide them with an imperfect product because it at least works and serves their purposes overall. They much prefer an imperfect solution to continuous talk about what I am going to do when all the planets align. But each next step has to be a more perfect product so that you retain trust. Bold and fearless does not mean foolish, but it is easy to recognize foolish. I am amazed at the number of association education providers who say, "we are going to be doing *a* live seminar this year." Get on with it. Jump out there. Think big. In the association e-learning business, if you are only going to do one seminar, you might as well not do any.

THE DABBLER'S DOWNFALL

While getting to the point of putting offerings into the market and then learning from the results is critical, it's relatively easy to never even get to that point. Many of the tools and approaches I reference in this book, for example, have been available for a number of years now. Even so, few people or organizations benefit at the level they could from them. They get excited about the possibilities and dabble around the edges in using some of the strategies and tactics described here. They may not fail outright, but they also don't succeed to any great degree. That is the main issue I see with people who are ultimately dissatisfied with these approaches. Like any entrepreneurial effort, success requires a certain level of focus and commitment. Just dabbling won't get you very far.

Dabbling is different from being in beta. If you are in beta, you have not only shipped; you are actively learning and evolving. Dabblers may never truly ship, and they aren't dedicated to learning and growing. They play with the tools. They start various initiatives, but never carry them through. The new business never really gets off the ground. The old ways of doing things never really change, and eventually everything just goes back to the way it was.

In most cases, dabblers know they need to embrace the tools and approaches I describe in this book, but as Jeffrey Pfeffer and Robert Sutton suggest in their bestselling book *The Knowing-Doing Gap: How Smart Companies Turn Knowledge into Action,* knowing is not enough. Pfeffer and Sutton argue that a lack of knowledge very rarely is the core reason why businesses are not as successful as they might be. Most organizations know, or can know, the same things. The difference is that some organizations manage to translate the knowledge they have into meaningful action. For the successful organizations with which I have worked, this has included:[1]

+ **Overcoming planning paralysis.** This is the essence of the beta mentality. Organizations that don't want to get bogged down in dabbling commit to shipping a minimum viable product and then actively learning.

+ **Overcoming "we have always done it that way" syndrome.** Repetition is essential for learning, but it is also a powerful force for stagnation. Doing what has been done in the past helps eliminate ambiguity and feels safe, but organizations that rely too heavily on past practices can't possibly move into the future.

+ **Overcoming complacence.** A sense that "all is okay" can reinforce the "we have always done it that way" mentality. Many organizations, for example, rely heavily on post-session evaluations to assess the state of their offerings and, by extension, their business. But this is a limited, if not flawed, approach. These valuations measure only what a learner is feeling at the point in time immediately following delivery of the learning experience. This information says almost nothing about the longer-term value of the experience, the "return on investment" the learner gets from it, how the experience compares to competing offerings, or what the learner's perception of the organization is likely to be the next time an educational offering rolls around. Organizations that pat themselves on the back simply because they receive good session evaluations may be blissfully marching their way to irrelevance.

+ **Breaking down silos.** I have consulted with organization after organization in which a separation of key functions like education, technology, and marketing made anything other than dabbling, or at best a half-hearted beta process, practically inevitable. As should be clear throughout this book, there can no longer be any significant separation of these three functions—whether within an organization or within the mind of a solo entrepreneur—for learning providers that expect to succeed.

Finally, one of the keys to bringing all of these elements together is having leaders who are insistent on talk becoming action. Over the years, I have seen many organizations attempt to launch and grow online education programs. With rare exception, the successful ones succeed not because they necessarily have the best products or the most innovative strategy, but because they have leaders who don't allow excuses for why things can't be done and who make sure processes are in place for following up on ideas. In short, they execute.

MEASURING—AND LEARNING—AS YOU GO

As I've stressed repeatedly, getting off the mark and getting offerings into the market is essential, but learning and evolving is equally essential. You want to create a culture of impact, not just execution. The only way you learn is by continually receiving and analyzing feedback on your efforts. While there are many ways of determining how your offerings are received and their ultimate impact, I'd argue there are two that trump all others in the context of marketing and selling educational experiences:

1. How many of the people who sign up for your learning experiences participate in more than one (or stay subscribed, in the case of ongoing communities) and continue to do so over time?

2. How many of the new people who participate in your learning experiences do so based on referrals from current learners?

Whether you do it formally (e.g., by surveying or tracking referral codes) or informally (e.g., by observation), determine whether your learners are coming back, and how regularly they do so. Ask how your new customers found you. There simply are no better measures of whether you are creating significant value than customers who believe you are creating significant value, who return consistently, and who spread the word to other potential customers.

These are, of course, *lagging* measures. By the time you know whether you are achieving the results you would like with them—including the associated financial results—it could easily be too late to correct course. So, it is also important to establish and track some key *leading* measures. This is where the concepts like the value continuum (Chapter 4) and "listening" (Chapter 2) come in again. If you have been following my advice in those two chapters, you are already set up to gauge your performance and determine what kind of impact you are having in your marketplace. Things to look and listen for include these:

◆ Are you consistently providing high-value options across all parts of your Accelerant Curve?

◆ Are you seeing consistent movement along the curve—i.e., does someone who starts at the top progress down the curve, whether smoothly or in "bounces"?

◆ Are elements of your curve being referenced and shared on blogs, social networks, and other web channels?

◆ Do learners talk about your paid experiences before, during, and after on platforms like Twitter, LinkedIn, Facebook, or their blogs?

I'm sure you can think of other possible clues to look for using some of the tools covered earlier in the book (see Chapters 2 and 5). In general, you want to see that community is developing, that context is building, and that your learners derive value from the defined, structured learning experiences you offer, but also that they are not confining their enthusiasm or their learning to the time and place of those experiences.

EVALUATING IMPACT

All of the previously mentioned measures provide insight into how you are performing from a business perspective and they also suggest, at least indirectly, that you are facilitating learning results that are of value to your audience. For some learning providers this level of measurement is sufficient, but in many cases, it is necessary to go further in measuring actual educational impact. With competition growing and continuing downward pressure on employer education and training budgets, the need to show impact is likely to grow. Over the past decade, there has been an increasing "buzz" in the corporate training sector about return on investment (ROI). Training departments are under pressure (or at least perceive themselves as under pressure) to demonstrate that investments in training and development result in actual bottom-line returns for the organizations. Whether or not this focus on ROI has produced significant results is debatable, but it seems inevitable that it will eventually trickle over into the continuing education and professional development market. As a result, I believe there is an opportunity for learning providers who want to distinguish themselves in their markets to get ahead of the curve.

Traditionally, one of the key ways that continuing education and professional development providers have measured impact is to issue and collect evaluations at the end of seminars, conference sessions, and other learning events. While a great deal of effort tends to be put into this process, it is ultimately of limited value from both a business and an educational perspective. Throughout years of consulting, I've seen any number of organizations receive top ratings on their evaluations from learners who do not participate in more than one conference or seminar a year with them, and may or may not return the next year. Good evaluations, in these cases, prove to be a poor predictor of ongoing business performance and sustainability. The problem is that evaluations are typically designed only to measure the reaction of learners to the learning experience, and a learner's reaction immediately following a learning experience does not necessarily correlate to the longer-term value the learner will derive.

As it happens, this is an issue that also ties into measuring learning impact. "Reaction" is Level I of the model for evaluation created by Robert Kirkpatrick and widely used throughout the world of adult training and education. Unfortunately this is, as Donald Clark put it, the "only part of Kirkpatrick's four levels that has failed to uphold to scrutiny over time."[2] A range of research has shown that there is little connection between the way people initially react to training or education and how it ultimately affects their performance. Indeed, there have been numerous situations in which instructors and sessions have received poor Level 1 evaluations and yet proved to have significant positive impact on learners' longer-term performance.

While it's unlikely that the emphasis on Level I "reaction" evaluations will go away anytime soon, there are practical steps that learning providers can take to start establishing potentially more meaningful measures of learning impact. These range from the informal and unscientific to the highly formal and scientific. I think approaches on both ends of the range have their value.

Support Meaningful Self-Assessment

The first step is to offer more opportunities for learners to assess their own learning and to do this in a way that the learning provider can track. While assessments are generally a part of formal credentialing and certification offerings, the vast majority of conferences and seminars do not offer meaningful assessment opportunities, and many e-learning experiences offer only nontracked self-tests or attendance/attention checks. The line of thinking on this seems to be that adults do not want to be tested, but I would argue that most adults *do* appreciate knowing whether they have successfully acquired new knowledge or skills, particularly if assessment is done in nonstressful, low-stakes manner. The Mozilla Open Badges project (http://openbadges.org/en-US/), which provides a framework for recognizing knowledge and skills obtained outside of traditional educational settings, might be seen as a model for facilitating this type of assessment.

Naturally, providing assessment to go along with learning experiences that do not currently include them would require additional effort, but it is effort that is likely to raise the value of the experience by enforcing a focus on objectives. In addition, assuming that learners do actually perform well on the assessments, providers who embrace this approach would have at least some assurance that concrete value is being delivered. There is no reason why this approach could not include both an assessment available prior to a learning event (pre-assessment) and an assessment available after (post-assessment). This would provide further evidence that the learning experience contributed to the learners' improvement.

There are a number of reasons, of course, why this is not a particularly scientific approach. Participation would most likely need to be self-selecting—that is, people would not be compelled to take an assessment. Moreover, there would normally be no "control group" to help filter out other variables that might contribute to a change in the learners' knowledge or skills. Nonetheless, having *any* information about learner achievement would be a significant improvement over the current situation.

Qualitatively Track Perceived Return

An informal approach I often use when interviewing lifelong learners for clients is to ask each interviewee to describe what he considers to be a high return on investment for a training or education experience. Based on that description, I then ask the learner to rate, on a scale from 1 to 10, how high he would rate the client organization on consistently providing that level of return. In many cases, interviewing as few as ten to fifteen learners in this way results in a fairly consistent picture of the level of educational value the organization delivers and allows establishment of a benchmark ROI rating. This same exercise can then be repeated annually or at other regular interviews to gauge change. My preference is to allow the learner to define ROI both initially and in follow-up interviews, because this helps the organization understand better what actually constitutes a good return in the minds of members and customers. Like the previous approach, this one is not terribly scientific, and yet it can yield incredibly valuable insights. Moreover, if the feedback on ROI is highly positive, and/or it grows year over year, this is information that can be shared as part of the learning provider's marketing efforts.

Quantitatively Track Return

As noted earlier, many organizations rely solely on reaction-oriented evaluations—Kirkpatrick's Level I—to gauge the impact of their educational programs. But there are three other levels of the Kirkpatrick model—learning, behavior, and results—and whether this or another evaluation model is used, it is certainly possible to track not just reaction, but actual changes in behavior and performance that result from educational experiences. Based on both my experience and my research for this book, it seems clear that assessment at levels higher than Level I (or some equivalent) is relatively rare in the world of lifelong learning, but it does happen. Particularly in the world of medicine and healthcare, where there is a growing emphasis on performance improvement to support overall quality improvement, there have been a number of instances in which the degree to which new knowledge and skills are used, and with what results, has been tracked. The basic design of these types of evaluations requires assessment prior to the learning experience, assessment after the learning experiences, and the cooperation of the learner and/or management at an organization in conducting follow-on assessments, interviews, and other types of evaluation activities over an extended period of time.

Clearly, given the resources and time commitments involved, this is not an exercise to be undertaken lightly. However, I think learning providers will increasingly need to undertake this kind of evaluation with at least some of their offerings to prove to learners and employers that the promised value is being delivered and also to allow the providers to learn much more than most of them know right now about what really works for serving their customers in a rapidly changing world.

FROM IMPACT TO INNOVATION

When you start evaluating impact, you've really come full circle to the core questions you asked when initially assessing your market. If your goal was to help the learner achieve high value and positive results, the question now is *did that happen?* If the answer is no, you have work to do to change the answer. If the answer is yes, the next question—after deserved self-congratulation—is *how can we provide more, better, or different value?*

It is from the perspective of value that any serious discussion of innovation has to flow. You started with a theory of value—that is, how you were going to improve the circumstances of your customers by delivering learning experiences. Now, you have evidence on which to base new theories of value. If you aren't basing your new initiatives—whether that means implementing new technologies or developing entirely new programs—on this kind of evidence, you are simply rolling the dice. The combination of a beta mentality, the approaches described throughout this book for assessing and engaging your audience, and, finally, actual measurement of impact, help ensure educated, high-probability bets that will lead to a growing, thriving business.

To explore the concept of innovation further, I talked with Seth Kahan, author of the bestselling book Getting Change Right *and a highly regarded expert on change and innovation. Seth laid out four key opportunities for innovation among many possibilities.*

One of the things that is so exciting about today's marketplace is that we're really limited only by the imagination. I'll give you an example of just four opportunities. One is what I'd call "never before exploited synergies," where you have the possibility of partnering or putting your product or service in combination with another product or service that was previously impossible. Or the cost of doing it was prohibitive and now it's easy to do it. So, for example, if you're an education provider there are tools now that are available over the Internet for free that you can couple with your work. I've seen people, for example, put together resource pages on the web or include them in documentation to lead people to what used to be considered avant-garde but are now established resources like Wikipedia.

Another approach is what I would call "emerging properties in an optimum combination." When you bring things together that have never been together before there will start to be new ways of using them, new qualities that emerge in the marketplace. I see people harvesting those. An example of that would be putting together a learning tool or learning set with apps on an iPhone and then being able to carry those apps into a particular work situation where they can be put to use in real time.

Another is the desire to improve bad customer experience. That always drives people, and there's still a great dearth of quality customer experience out there. When I talk about customer experience I'm really talking about a multistage journey every time the customer interfaces with a particular company. I'm not just talking about the point of a financial transaction. I've mapped eleven different stages that a customer goes through in interfacing with a particular organization, and at every one of those there's an opportunity for a high level of quality experience. Many organizations are still very much involved in what I would call customer service, which is responding to a problem that has arisen *after* the adoption of the product or service. That's only one of the touch points; there are ten other touch points. People who are paying attention to that typically tend to be leaders in their field.

The last one I would raise—and there are many more than these four—are changing market trends. We're in an economy that's moving all around us and there are things that are surging, things that are ebbing, and if you think of your product or service in relation to that shift, different aspects of it are emphasized. For example, I know of a company that was providing education to real estate salespeople in Florida. When the market tanked all of a sudden, all of their customers were out of a job. One hundred percent of them were out of a job. They [the company] had no customer base. But actually they did have connections to the individuals they'd been serving even though they were no longer buying real estate supplies or coming to real estate classes. And so they quickly mobilized and began teaching classes that were providing techniques for those very same people to generate income while they were going through the gap. As a result they held on to their entire customer base through the drought in the market. So, if you are someone who at one point was providing real estate education, suddenly the real estate disappears and you ask, "Well, what asset do I have?" And the asset that you have is the connection with your customer base and the ability to deliver education even if the content has changed 180 degrees.

Get the full interview with Seth at www.learning-revolution.net/podcast/.

NOTES

1. These points, which are drawn from many years of working with continuing education clients, are consistent with key aspects of the "knowing-doing gap" as described by Pfeffer and Sutton.

2. Donald Clark, "Kirkpatrick's four level evaluation model," *Big Dog & Little Dog's Performance Juxtaposition*, http://www.nwlink.com/~donclark/hrd/isd/kirkpatrick.html. Retrieved July 7, 2012.

CHAPTER 10

TAKING IT TO THE NEXT LEVEL: LEADING LEARNING

THE STRATEGIES AND TACTICS covered in this book should be of significant help to anyone with the expertise, or access to the expertise, to develop and grow a successful education business. However, I believe the opportunity is much larger than simply delivering educational experiences in the traditional sense. As I have noted numerous times throughout this book, we live in a world in which knowledge evolves at a faster pace than ever and where an ability to learn continually and rapidly is one of the most valuable skills individuals and organizations can possess. In this context, organizations or individuals that are able to point the way, to help others make sense and excel in their chosen fields and interests, play a unique and highly valuable role. In short, those who are able to lead learning will lead their chosen field, industry, or area of knowledge.

FROM CATALOG TO PLATFORM

One of the shifts in thinking at the core of this book is moving away from focusing on single products or experiences confined to a particular time span to thinking instead about the way in which the needs of learners will evolve over a lifetime and how you may be able to support a range of needs across a long span of time. This kind of thinking leads naturally to an emphasis on context and community and also encourages you to think of your education business holistically as a *platform* for connecting and engaging with learners over time. While a platform may provide access to all of the standard classes, courses, and other types of content that have traditionally been the focus of education businesses, it is fundamentally different at its core. I like the way John Jantsch, author of *Duct Tape Marketing* and founder of the very popular blog and podcast series with the same name, describes platform thinking. "The notion," Jantsch says,

> is that your business can be so much more than a group of products and services. Truly great businesses are now viewed not only as a group of products and services, but also as a place where people can go to work to build things they are passionate about.

You can't *make* people "go to work" in this way any more than you can make them learn. They have to be intrinsically motivated. You simply provide the context and the community where this motivation can blossom.

While I have emphasized technology throughout this book, I hope it is clear that in using the term "platform" I do not mean a technology platform. Technology is an enabler—a very powerful one—for individuals and organizations that want to create a platform. It provides a tool set for making platform thinking real. But as anyone with a low-traffic website, unused discussion forum, or paltry list of Twitter followers knows, technology does nothing other than open the doors. You have to fill the seats. A better point of reference, particularly given the leadership focus of this book and this chapter, might be a political platform. Political platforms succeed or fail based on how well they tap into the intrinsic motivations of their adherents. They encompass a variety of different content and experiences, from banners and slogans to position papers to rallies. They offer a channel for a shared vision and goals, but the best ones also take a "big tent" approach that allows for a significant amount of diversity and even disagreement among participants. At the same time, political platforms cannot be without substance, any more than a learning community can be without substance, or they ultimately founder. Leaders provide some of the substance, but more important, they elicit contributions from others.

SHIFTING POWER TO LEARNERS

Just as political platforms are often about bringing more "power to the people," learning platforms should support learners in being as successful with their learning as possible. This is not as simple, however, as giving people access to content and tools to collaborate and communicate among themselves. There is ample reason to believe that many of us— perhaps most of us—need some help in becoming the learners we are capable of being. This, in my opinion, is an opportunity for leadership.

Malcolm Knowles, widely regarded as *the* leading thinker in the world of adult education, touched on this problem in the later editions of his seminal work, *The Adult Learner.* Knowles first introduced his concept of andragogy in 1970, but it was not until 1995—two years before he died—that he and his collaborators added the step of "preparing the learner" to his theory of adult learning. This was largely a response to issues he saw with "self-concept." Here's a relevant passage from the discussion of self-concept in *The Adult Learner*:

> The minute adults walk into an activity labeled "education," or "training," or anything synonymous, they hark back to their conditioning in previous school experience, put on their dunce hats of dependency, fold their arms, sit back, and say "teach me." This assumption of required dependency and the facilitator's subsequent treatment of adult students as children creates a conflict within them between their intellectual model—learner equals dependent—and the deeper, perhaps subconscious, psychological need to be self-directing. And the typical method of dealing

with psychological conflict is to try to flee from the situation caus-
ing it, which probably accounts in part for the high dropout rate in
much voluntary adult education.[1]

The bottom line is that, while there are many exciting ways to create
more interactive and participatory learning than is often encountered in,
say, your average conference session, there is ample reason to believe that
most of us are not particularly well prepared to engage in and benefit
from such learning. To a very large extent—as *The Adult Learner* suggests—this is a vestige of K–12 education systems based largely on passive learning experiences. In the United States, it can also, no doubt, be
attributed to what Dr. Monisha Pasupathi, associate professor in developmental psychology at the University of Utah, referenced in my interview with her for this book as the "anti-intellectual tradition" in
American culture. I see a number of implications in this situation and a
corresponding number of opportunities for learning leaders:

◆   Learning providers can't assume "self-directedness" on the part
of their learners. While there is a good chance that the core group of
highly motivated learners within any market will be self-directed, the
broader audience may need some guidance in how to take advantage of
self-directed learning. Moreover, even learners who are already highly
self-directed most likely need instruction on effective learning strategies.

◆   If most adults are constrained by their pedagogical baggage, then
it is hardly likely that they will be able to tell your organization what a
great learning experience looks like. In other words, asking if they will
like "X" or "Y" type of experiences is not likely to be all that helpful—
and it may, in fact, keep you from pursuing the best strategies. Learning
providers must be prepared to take some risks, make some leaps, to lead
their learners to new and better places. This sort of thinking, of course,
is at the heart of the experimentation and learning approaches that I
advocate throughout this book.

◆   The two previous points notwithstanding, learning providers
must recognize that there are many individuals who are self-directed and

intrinsically motivated and who essentially bring their own problem-solving and task-oriented processes to each learning experience. For these learners, content-centered learning experiences may often be preferable to collaborative or community-oriented learning experiences. Similarly, traditional lecture-type experiences and reading remain essential for sharing foundational knowledge with novice learners. The varying levels of prior knowledge and learning skills among learners is yet another reason why providing options along your value continuum is so important.

Finally, it seems likely that the problematic side of "self-concept" is diminished if you remove the obvious, traditional labels like "seminar" or "webinar." It's telling that many of the successful initiatives I highlight in this book—The A-list Blogger Club or the massive multiplayer games from the Institute for the Future, for example—do not label themselves as traditional educational activities. A lack of such labels is also a key reason why social networks are often very powerful as learning environments; people tend not to consciously acknowledge them as such even though learning is typically *the* key social object in any professional community that survives and thrives over time. Educators must recognize this and learn to facilitate learning within networks if they want to truly lead learning in their fields and industries.

Return on Shift

Empowering learners is core to the idea of leading learning because of the tremendous value potential it represents. In "The Amazing Era of Self-Service Learning," Patricia McLagan argues that, in the world of corporate training, there is a significant opportunity in supporting learners with their self-managed learning activities. "If we could help learners manage their learning," McLagan writes,

> I speculate that there would be as much as a 500 percent increase in benefits due to clearer intentions, selection of better resources, better information processing and concentration, more focused

learning, greater learning transfer, and ultimately better results. Also, the more we know about that learner-led dynamic, the better we can support it both as learning professionals and informal helpers.[2]

There's no doubt that "500 percent" is bold speculation, but I'm on board with it, and I think this line of reasoning applies at least as much to the continuing education and professional development market as it does to corporate training. McLagan notes that

> There are important areas where self-managed learning breaks down. People have trouble, for example, clarifying what they want to learn. They don't always use the best resources. Their information-processing skills can be improved. They don't really know what the process is to develop a new skill or to rise above an outmoded attitude, belief, or value. People run into plateaus and obstacles and get discouraged or quit. They don't always use third-party help in the best possible way. And learners don't declare victory when they have achieved a learning goal; rather, they blur one learning project into another as one learning project fades and others begin.

These are areas where it is well within the reach of the average learning provider to give support, and clues to that support are contained in the passage quoted. It's not too difficult, for example, to imagine your average trade or professional association kicking off each new year with a series of articles, webinars, videos, or (preferably) some combination of these things dedicated to:

- Clarifying your personal learning goals for the year
- Finding and making use of key resources available from your association
- Learning effective processes for developing new skills and habits
- Effectively tapping the knowledge and skills of your peers

- Overcoming obstacles and celebrating your learning victories
- Implementing and sustaining new skills and knowledge

Similar issues could be included in an orientation package the first time a learner purchases a course or seminar, or upon registration for a learning community site. While I mainly have informal and self-managed learning in mind, I also can see addressing the topics in the preceding list in the opening session at a conference or other learning event. Such an event might then wrap up with a well-facilitated session in which attendees review and reflect upon both their formal and informal learning at the conference.

The bottom line is that there is significant value to be generated through better equipping adult learners to learn. For learning providers, actively supporting this process can lead to higher-value, longer-term relationships with customers and members.

I asked George Siemens, whose pioneering efforts with "massive open online courses" were covered in Chapter 3, to share his perspectives on how well we are prepared for the new world of learning in which we live. Here's what he had to say:

On the one hand, I think human beings are naturally meaning-makers. We try to see how pieces in the world connect and we explore. As Pirelli has stated, this is a concept of information foraging. We treat information almost like we treat food biologically. It is something that we pursue and it is something that we apprehend and we categorize; we connect pieces. So that itself is not new. Trying to form coherence out of fragmentation is hardly a new human activity driven by the online environment.

What is new is that the flow of information is at a pace that we can't cognitively handle anymore and probably haven't been able to for a century or more. Certainly today it's very pronounced. That means that these methods that we've used in the past simply don't work as well, and so as a result of that, even though we are skilled sense-makers, what we started to look at today is alternative means of doing that.

So, while we're socially capable of sense-making, very capable of it, it's the scale that throws us for a loop. That's where we do face some challenges because individuals have to alter some of their expectations. For example, an open online course—one of the first things we find is that students are completely overwhelmed because they're trying to read everything. They're treating it like a traditional course where someone has created a bounded structure around it and they have to read everything.

In [the case of a MOOC] a big part of the initial stage of the course is to let learners know that you can't read everything . . . you can't comment on everything, you can't track all the conversations. What you do instead is you skim. You find the bits and pieces that are relevant to you. You begin to form, as I mentioned earlier, sub-networks or systems that you have control of that you're able to personalize.

These are skills that not everyone has. In fact, with almost all learners that we've had, we know what's going to happen the first two weeks. The conversation is almost identical as we're trying to let learners know that you can't master all of this. You have to be selective in your reading. You have to learn how to extract important elements. You have to connect to networks, social networks, to make sense of it. You have to rely on technical systems to archive and make sense of the important information. And the list goes on.

LEADING LEARNING, LEADING CHANGE

A great deal can happen when long-term, high-value relationships are forged among a group of people. At its core, learning is a process of change—change in knowledge, in skills, in behavior. A learning platform—in the sense that I use the word "platform" in this chapter—can become a cauldron of change over time, a place where new knowledge, skills, and behaviors extend beyond the individual to create change that impacts an entire group or community. Learning providers who create platforms become change agents and put themselves in a position to lead change. In essence, this is social learning in its most powerful form. As an article in *Ecology and Society*[3] puts it, social learning of this type:

◆ Occurs through social interactions and processes between actors within a social network

◆ Facilitates change in the individuals involved

◆ Becomes situated within wide units or communities of practice

While not all social learning may lead to the broader change suggested by the third bullet, the fact that it *can* has tremendous strategic implications for learning providers and the role they can potentially play for their audiences. A key implication, I believe, is that organizations need to pull back and look at the full range of educational options they offer and consider the broader learning conversations to which they connect. Are the seminars, webinars, conferences, online courses, and other learning experiences you offer isolated events, or do they tie tightly into a broader vision for how and where you might lead your members and customers? How do the less formal elements of your contact with audience—blog posts, posts on social networks, tweets—help to tie together the formal educational elements and contribute to an overall vision? Are you supporting your learners in taking full advantage of what the tools and opportunities of the new learning landscape offer? How, ultimately, are you having an impact?

In my experience, this is not how most of us in the world of lifelong learning think about our work. We need to, though. We've got a revolution to lead.

NOTES

1. Elwood F. Holton III, Malcolm Knowles, and Richard A. Swanson, *The adult learner: The definitive classic in adult education and*

human resource development (Taylor & Francis, Kindle Edition), Chapter 4: A Theory of Adult Learning, "The Andragogical Model."

2. Patricia McLagan, "The amazing era of self-service learning," *T+D*, December 2011, www.astd.org/Publications/Magazines/ TD/TD-Archive/2011/12/The-Ama zing-Era-of-Self-Service -Learning.

3. Mark S. Reed et al., "What is social learning?" *Ecology and Society* 15(4): r1. 2010 [online], www.ecologyandsociety.org/vol15/ iss4/resp1.

CREATING AN
ACTION PLAN

DEPENDING ON YOUR STARTING POINT, you may want to use different parts of this book at different times, but here's a general model for putting the pieces together.

1. FULLY UNDERSTAND YOUR MARKET: CHAPTERS 1 AND 2

Out of the five major forces discussed—economic, educational, technological, neuropsychological, generational—identify the ones currently having the most impact on your market or potential market. What opportunities are they creating?

What theories and assumptions do you have about the audience you aim to serve? These might include:

- ◆ Key characteristics and traits of your prospects
- ◆ Challenges and issues your prospects are facing and how they are dealing with them

- Knowledge and skill levels your prospects are likely to have
- Sources of motivation, especially intrinsic motivation

Go through the process of searching, listening, asking, and testing to check your theories and assumptions. Consider how the results:

- Confirm, refute, or alter your theories and assumptions
- Highlight new needs of which you may not have been aware
- Uncover competition you did not know existed
- Surface potential allies, distribution channels, or other valuable relationships

In general, what results can you deliver through education that will create positive, valuable change for this audience?

2. DETERMINE YOUR BUSINESS MODEL AND POSITIONING: CHAPTERS 3 AND 4

To develop your business model, articulate:

- Your value proposition

  How do factors like convenience and relevance apply?

- Resources (people, technologies, etc.) required to support the value proposition

  How important are factors like velocity and brand?

- Options for generating revenue

  How can you apply concepts like validation, intimacy, customization, and analytics?

What possibilities do the four models discussed—P^2 Communities, Flipped, Virtual Conference, and Massive—represent for your business? How might you follow or borrow from them?

How can you use the strategies discussed to be unique, memorable, and remarkable?

- Build on strengths
- Redefine the market
- Set the standard
- Be contrarian
- Create a story
- Imitate strategically
- Adapt creatively

What content and experiences will you provide along your Accelerant Curve?

Based on the value you are providing, how will you price along your Accelerant Curve?

3. DESIGN AND DEVELOP LEARNING EXPERIENCES: CHAPTERS 5 AND 6

Define clear objectives for your learning experiences that align with the overall value you aim to deliver. Remember, objectives should be specific and measurable.

Adhere to good practices in developing and delivering content. Be sure to:

- Position it
- Prune it
- Chunk it
- Stimulate multiple senses
- Remember to repeat to remember
- Make it active
- Share the responsibility

Determine how you might interact with your audience through informal and social learning channels. Which platforms will you use? Remember the principles of attention, interest, motivation, and outcomes.

What tools will you need in order to develop and deliver learning experiences that meet your audience's needs? Key development and delivery activities may include:

- Managing a web home base
- Shooting and editing digital video
- Recording screencasts
- Capturing and editing audio
- Doing basic image editing
- Hosting a webinar or webcast
- Creating nicely formatted documents
- Creating on-demand courses
- Deploying and managing a learning management system

4. STAY CONNECTED, PROMOTE, AND CONVERT: CHAPTERS 7 AND 8

What approaches will you take to providing valuable content to your market on an ongoing basis? These might include:

- Staying tuned in
- Curating value
- Conducting rapid research
- Writing it together

Put in place the tools and tactics that will help learners find you and enable you to communicate with them directly. These include:

- E-mail
- Search
- Social tools
- Video

Develop effective landing pages to convert prospective learners into actual customers.

5. EXECUTE FOR IMPACT AND CHANGE: CHAPTERS 9 AND 10

Identify barriers that might hold you or your organization back. How will you address them? Challenges might include:

- Overcoming planning paralysis
- Overcoming "we have always done it that way" syndrome
- Overcoming complacence
- Breaking down silos

Determine the approaches you will you take toward measuring the impact your learning experiences have. Will they be more or less formal?

What opportunities do you see for shifting power to learners?

What broader positive change will you strive to lead with your platform?

INDEX